Horizon

NOVEMBER, 1963 · VOLUME V, NUMBER 8

Fifth-Anniversary Announcement

This year marks, for the editors of Horizon, an important anniversary: it was in 1958 that we launched this unusual magazine and promised, within its pages, ". . . to open the door, and serve as a guide—with all the wit and perception we can summon up—to the long cultural adventure of modern man."

At five, how well has Horizon done? How well has it fulfilled that promise? The answer is, in part, that we are known, quoted, argued with, and praised around the world. Friendly critics have been kind enough to call us "a new kind of continuing liberal education" and "the most beautiful magazine in existence." Horizon has grown from nothing to an average circulation of nearly 150,000. No periodical 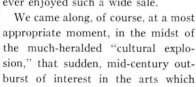 of comparable quality or price has ever enjoyed such a wide sale.

We came along, of course, at a most appropriate moment, in the midst of the much-heralded "cultural explosion," that sudden, mid-century outburst of interest in the arts which

John Canaday

has resulted from the unprecedented spread of education, wealth, and leisure. Never before have so many painters painted, sculptors sculpted, or writers written; never before have so many techniques of mass reproduction and distribution been so highly developed. Movements seem to make their way around the world in a moment, and fads almost fly. The problem for educated people, therefore, be-

comes one not of availability but of discrimination and quality, of choosing the significant and the enduring out of all this chaotic outpouring. It is Horizon's task to make selections like this in every issue, and to present our choices from all this vast cultural storehouse, past and present, in the most interesting way we know.

Our anniversary, we think, is a good opportunity to take a few steps forward. Evidence has been accumulating that Horizon, for all those devoted 150,000 subscribers, has not reached its full potential size—and that a great many more people would take the magazine if the price, which is steep, could be reduced. But that, as we told readers in a recent letter, is no easy matter. When you scour the earth for the best authors, for the best works of art, for the finest in paper, printing, and binding—and when costs, as everyone knows, go only up—how do you go about a price reduction? Cut size? Reduce the quality? Accept advertising? We like these proposals no more than our readers would.

The sensible solution, we concluded, is to publish a little more magazine a little less often, quarterly instead of bimonthly. Our first quarterly number will be the next one, to be delivered in January. New and renewal prices will be substantially lower, and subscribers on the old bimonthly basis will receive the full number of copies they have purchased. The format and size will be unchanged, although the quarterly

PUBLISHER: James Parton   EDITORIAL DIRECTOR: Joseph J. Thorndike, Jr.
SENIOR EDITOR: William Harlan Hale   MANAGING EDITOR: Eric Larrabee

ASSOCIATE EDITOR: Ralph Backlund   ASSISTANT EDITORS: Jane Wilson, Albert Bermel, Shirley Abbott
CONTRIBUTING EDITOR: Margery Darrell   EDITORIAL ASSISTANTS: Wendy Buehr, Priscilla Flood
LIBRARIAN: Caroline Backlund   COPY EDITOR: Mary Ann Pfeiffer
ASSISTANT COPY EDITORS: Joan Rehe, Ruth H. Wolfe

SENIOR ART DIRECTOR: Irwin Glusker   ART DIRECTOR: Elton Robinson

ADVISORY BOARD: Gilbert Highet, *Chairman*, Frederick Burkhardt, Marshall B. Davidson,
Richard M. Ketchum, Oliver Jensen, Jotham Johnson, John Walker

EUROPEAN CONSULTING EDITOR: J. H. Plumb, *Christ's College, Cambridge*
EUROPEAN BUREAU: Gertrudis Feliu, *Chief, 11 rue du Bouloi, Paris Ier*

HORIZON
A Magazine of the Arts

NOVEMBER, 1963 · VOLUME V, NUMBER 8

will contain a few more pages than, for example, this issue, in order to provide more color illustration.

HORIZON will continue to devote itself, as before, to art and thought and history, tracing the roots of our many-faceted culture up to our own times. A new program, however, envisages organizing the coverage of certain key subjects in such a way as to make more obvious and vital the continuing value of the magazine. We are commencing, for example, a number of new series. One, conducted and written for us by the eminent art critic John Canaday, will be devoted to *Great Artists and Their Worlds;* heavily illustrated, often in fine gravure, it will continue regularly until the subscriber has collected, in effect, a good art library. Similarly we plan a series on architects, another on noted men of letters, and a third on those philosophers and men of science who have reshaped the modern world. We call the last of these *Makers of Modern Thought,* and launch it with a singularly poetic essay by Dr. Loren Eiseley, of the University of Pennsylvania, on the life and ideas of Francis Bacon, the inventor of the experimental method, "that means by which all things else may be discovered."

Loren Eiseley

With such additions to our contents, we hope you will agree more than ever with the reader who said of us last year, "HORIZON says what civilization is."

THE EDITORS

HORIZON is published every two months by American Heritage Publishing Co., Inc. Executive and editorial offices: 551 Fifth Ave., New York 17, N.Y. HORIZON welcomes contributions but can assume no responsibility for unsolicited material.

All correspondence about subscriptions should be addressed to: HORIZON Subscription Office, 379 West Center St., Marion, Ohio.

Single Copies: $4.50
Annual Subscriptions: $21.00 in the U.S. & Can.
$22.00 elsewhere

Starting in January, 1964, HORIZON will be published quarterly at the annual rate of $16.00 in the U.S. and Canada ($17.00 elsewhere).

Annual indexes for Volumes I–IV priced at $1 have been published every September. The index for Volume V will be published in March, 1964, as will a cumulative index for Volumes I–V priced at $3. HORIZON is also indexed in the *Readers Guide to Periodical Literature.*

Title registered U.S. Patent Office

Second-class postage paid at New York, N.Y., and at additional mailing offices.

COVER: Under his heavy crown, the heavy-lidded eyes of Justinian look out at us from the walls of San Vitale in Ravenna, Italy. He was the greatest of the Byzantine rulers, and his portrait is, appropriately, one of the greatest examples of Byzantine art. An article on Byzantium begins on page 4.

BYZANTIUM: THE OTHER HALF OF THE WORLD

The achievement of the Byzantines (who called themselves "Romans") was to keep barbarians at bay, create a new art, preserve Western culture for a thousand years, and push a little further the limits of both piety and depravity

By PHILIP SHERRARD

It is only recently that the word "Byzantium" has been freed from the contumely attached to it by several generations of uncomprehending, humanist-minded historians. Pre-eminent among them was Edward Gibbon, for whom Byzantine history was "a tedious and uniform tale of weakness and misery" in which "not a single discovery was made to exalt the dignity or promote the happiness of mankind." Christian Byzantium—or rather the triumph of Christianity itself—marked for Gibbon the end of the "classical" civilization he so much admired, marked indeed the decline and fall of the Roman Empire. At the end of his vast work he notes modestly: "I have described the triumph of barbarism and religion."

Some hundred years later another historian, William Lecky, was still echoing Gibbon's contempt: "Of that By-

zantine Empire, the universal verdict of history is that it constitutes, without a single exception, the most thoroughly base and despicable form that civilization has yet assumed. . . . [It] is a monotonous story of the intrigues of priests, eunuchs, and women, of poisonings, of conspiracies, of uniform ingratitude, of perpetual fratricides."

Judgments like this, which could be multiplied, are not likely to be made today, or to carry much weight if they are. Byzantine history and civilization have become legitimate

Constantine the Great humbly offers a model of the city of Constantinople to the Virgin in this detail of a tenth-century mosaic in Hagia Sophia. The Emperor issued an edict of toleration for Christianity in A.D. 313, but it is a matter of historical debate whether he was ever converted to the faith.

4

objects of academic attention. There are now institutes, such as that at Dumbarton Oaks in Washington, where notable scholars devote themselves entirely to the gathering, sifting, and assessing of Byzantine material. As a result, Byzantine society is no longer regarded as the stagnant playground of decadent voluptuaries, immersed in sensuality and bestirring themselves only when provoked by some outburst of public spleen in the Hippodrome, or by some hair-splitting theological subtlety thrown into their midst by fanatic monks. In art, literature, statesmanship, diplomacy, and war, Byzantium's achievements are now recognized, even admired. The philosopher Alfred North Whitehead went so far as to assert that its culture was superior to that of classical Rome, and some distinguished historians have claimed that it afforded greater opportunities for living a civilized life than the Pax Augusta. It might in fact seem that the wheel has come full circle, and that Gibbon's thesis is being reversed: it is no longer a question of Rome's decline and fall, but of Byzantium's ascent and triumph.

For in fact the Byzantine Empire was not simply the Roman Empire extended in a semiparalytic state through another thousand-odd years of slow ossification and decay.

This was a new creation, growing out of the Roman past but essentially different from it. Indeed, it was precisely a failure of ideology in the Empire of the Caesars that made a new form of society imperative if Western civilization was to survive. Already in the second century A.D. the Roman Empire was threatened with disruption. There were civil wars within and frontier wars without; legions mutinied, Goths and Parthians bestirred themselves. The highly centralized administrative machinery creaked under the strain. Disaster was averted for the time being by Diocletian, who came to power in A.D. 284. He introduced a series of measures to decentralize and stabilize the Empire, now split for this purpose into four great compartments. But these reforms only postponed matters, for after his death, as after the death of Alexander the Great, struggles broke out between the rulers of the various parts of the Empire as they contended for the imperial throne. And it was only in A.D. 323 that the triumphant survivor was able to take the steps that ultimately created the empire of the Byzantines.

*T*his survivor was Constantine, known to history because of the magnitude of his achievements as Constantine the Great. He was born in Moesia, the province of the modern Serbs and Bulgars, and as a youth was sent to the court of Nicomedia in Asia Minor, which Diocletian had already chosen for his headquarters in preference to Rome. After serving in Persia and Egypt, he was acclaimed Caesar at York, in England, where his father had died while on a punitive expedition against the Scots. The next six years Constantine spent in Gaul and Italy as co-emperor with Maxentius, and in A.D. 312 he captured Rome from his colleague. This made him sole emperor in the West, with Licinius, sole emperor in the East, as his only rival. His final triumph did not come until A.D. 323 with the defeat and capture of Licinius, after a struggle into which both parties had thrown all their strength.

Faced now with the task of arresting the disintegration of the Empire and of welding its heterogeneous elements, both territorial and cultural, into a new coherence, Constantine made it his first concern to choose and construct a new imperial capital. Where should this be? Rome was the scene of conspiracy and intrigue, while to the north and west were lands of unreclaimed barbarity. The East seemed the obvious choice: there was the main focus of trade; it was there that some bulwark had to be found to resist the Parthians and

Though Constantine lies asleep in the top panel of this miniature (from a ninth-century manuscript of the homilies of Saint Gregory of Nazianzus), it was the turning point of his life: he had a vision of a flaming cross inscribed "In this sign conquer." Taking it as a portent, he marched on Rome and defeated his rival Maxentius at the Milvian bridge (center). In the bottom panel Constantine's mother, Saint Helena, makes her legendary discovery of the True Cross in Jerusalem.

ЄYPЄC
TOYT
IOYCT
POY

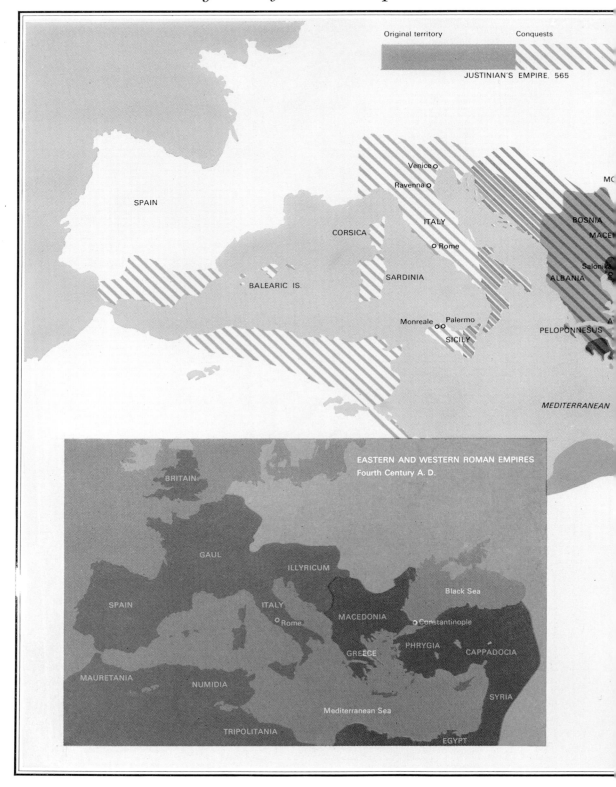

Original territory   Conquests

JUSTINIAN'S EMPIRE, 565

SPAIN

Venice o
Ravenna o

MO

BOSNIA
MACE

ITALY

CORSICA   o Rome

SARDINIA   Salonik
                                     ALBANIA

BALEARIC IS.

                    Monreale o o Palermo   PELOPONNESUS
                              SICILY

MEDITERRANEAN

EASTERN AND WESTERN ROMAN EMPIRES
Fourth Century A. D.

BRITAIN

GAUL
                    ILLYRICUM

                                      Black Sea

SPAIN   ITALY
               o Rome   MACEDONIA   o Constantinople

                            GREECE   PHRYGIA   CAPPADOCIA

MAURETANIA   NUMIDIA

                                              SYRIA

                    Mediterranean Sea

          TRIPOLITANIA   EGYPT

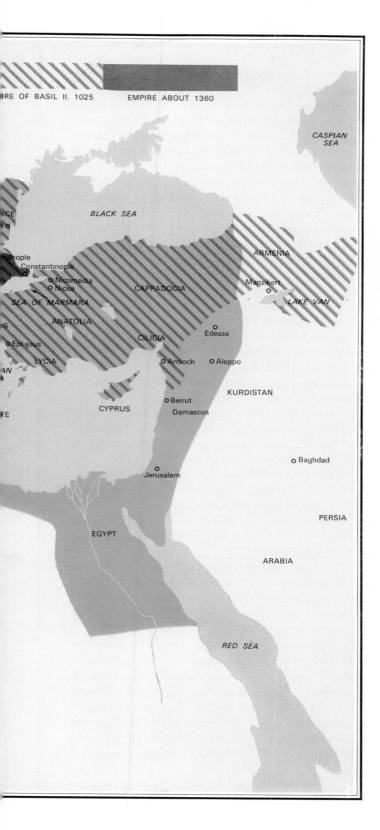

RE OF BASIL II, 1025   EMPIRE ABOUT 1360

CASPIAN SEA

BLACK SEA

ARMENIA

Constantinople
Nicomedia
Nicea
CAPPADOCIA
Manzikert
LAKE VAN
SEA OF MARMARA
ANATOLIA
CILICIA
Edessa
Ephesus
LYCIA
Antioch
Aleppo
KURDISTAN
CYPRUS
Beirut
Damascus
Baghdad
Jerusalem
PERSIA
EGYPT
ARABIA
RED SEA

to check the westerly migrations from the steppes; and it was there that Christianity was rapidly gaining an ascendancy sufficient to displace the dead or dying ideologies of the ancient world. And if the East was obvious, what better site could there be than the small town of Byzantium? Set on a triangular peninsula commanding the mouth of the Bosporus, which links the Sea of Marmara with the Black Sea and divides Europe from Asia, Byzantium seemed to meet all the requirements. The climate was cool and healthy. Along one side of the triangular peninsula was an inlet that formed a perfect natural harbor: the Golden Horn. To the south lay the Aegean and the rich gardens of Asia Minor, source of all the earth's fruits, and beyond, the flax fields of Egypt. To the east, as far as India and China, stretched the trade routes along which passed those treasured spices and medicaments—pepper and musk, cloves and nutmeg, cinnamon and camphor, sugar and ginger, aloes and balsam—that were to lend such refinement to the Byzantine cuisine; and thence, too, came the ivory and amber, pearls and precious stones, porcelain and glass, muslin, taffeta, and damask that were to be the raw materials of Byzantine reliquaries and embroideries. To the north lay Russia and those ports of the Black Sea through which flowed wheat and furs, honey and gold, wax and slaves. Byzantium's natural defenses were, as Constantine had discovered during the war with Licinius, as good as could be desired; and he must have sensed prodigious possibilities as he chose this site and marked out with his own hands the confines of the new city to which he gave his name, and which for more than a thousand years was to be the focus of Western civilization.

*M*aterials for its building were at hand in the marbles of Proconnesus, a nearby island, and in the wood from forests bordering the Black Sea. Edifice after imperial edifice began to rise on the spacious platform, once the ancient acropolis, of the peninsula that divided the Sea of Marmara from the still waters of the Golden Horn. To the east of this platform was the Senate House; to the south was the Great Palace, a dense group of buildings stretching through gardens down to the shore, where for many centuries stood the porphyry pavilion of the empresses; to the west lay the Forum and the vast theatre of the Hippodrome, capable of seating forty thousand people and containing works of art Constantine had rifled from the entire classical world: four great bronze horses (eventually removed to the façade of St. Mark's in Venice, where they remain to this day); the bronze eagle and Calydonian boar; the bronze triple pillar from Delphi, bearing the names of the thirty-one Greek states that had triumphed over the armies of the Persian Xerxes at Plataea in 479 B.C.; and much more. Northeast of the Hippodrome, on the headland most visible to ships approaching from the south, Constantine placed the Church of the Holy Wisdom, Hagia Sophia. Enlarged by his son Constantius and rebuilt in the sixth century by the emperor

The Emperor's Vices: A Cynical Byzantine Tells All

The chief historian of Justinian's day was Procopius, a courtier of rank and the author of an eight-volume work known as the Wars. *What the Emperor did not know was that Procopius was also writing a book called the* Secret Histories, *which he was filling with all the scandalous stories he had heard about Justinian and Theodora. The following excerpt is from Richard Atwater's translation, published by the University of Michigan Press in 1961:*

I think this is as good a time as any to describe the personal appearance of [Justinian]. Now in physique he was neither tall nor short, but of average height; not thin, but moderately plump; his face was round, and not bad looking, for he had good color, even when he fasted for two days. . . . Now such was Justinian in appearance; but his character was something I could not fully describe. For he was at once villainous and amenable; as people say colloquially, a moron. He was never truthful with anyone, but always guileful in what he said and did, yet easily hoodwinked by any who wanted to deceive him. His nature was an unnatural mixture of folly and wickedness. What in olden times a peripatetic philosopher said was also true of him, that opposite qualities combine in a man as in the mixing of colors. I will try to portray him, however, insofar as I can fathom his complexity.

This Emperor, then, was deceitful, devious, false, hypocritical, two-faced, cruel, skilled in dissembling his thought, never moved to tears by either joy or pain, though he could summon them artfully at will when the occasion demanded, a liar always, not only offhand, but in writing, and when he swore sacred oaths to his subjects in their very hearing. Then he would immediately break his agreements and pledges, like the vilest of slaves, whom indeed only the fear of torture drives to confess their perjury. A faithless friend, he was a treacherous enemy, insane for murder and plunder, quarrelsome and revolutionary, easily led to anything evil, but never willing to listen to good counsel, quick to plan mischief and carry it out, but finding even the hearing of anything good distasteful to his ears. . . .

[Justinian] took a wife: and in what manner she was born and bred, and, wedded to this man, tore up the Roman Empire by its very roots, I shall now relate.

Acacius was the keeper of wild beasts used in the amphitheatre in Constantinople; he belonged to the Green faction and was nicknamed the Bearkeeper. This man . . . died, leaving three daughters named Comito, Theodora, and Anastasia: of whom the eldest was not yet seven years old. . . .

When these children reached the age of girlhood, their mother put them on the local stage, for they were fair to look upon. . . . Theodora, the second sister, dressed in a little tunic with sleeves, like a slave girl, waited on Comito and used to follow her about. . . . But as soon as she arrived at the age of youth, and was now ready for the world, her mother put her on the stage. Forthwith, she became a courtesan, and such as the ancient Greeks used to call a common one, at that: for she was not a flute or harp player, nor was she even trained to dance, but only gave her youth to anyone she met, in utter abandonment. Her general favors included, of course, the actors in the theatre; and in their productions she took part in the low comedy scenes. For she was very funny and a good mimic, and immediately became popular in this art. There was no shame in the girl, and no one ever saw her dismayed: no role was too scandalous for her to accept without a blush.

. . . Any respectable man who chanced upon her in the Forum avoided her and withdrew in haste, lest the hem of his mantle, touching such a creature, might be thought to share in her pollution. For to those who saw her, especially at dawn, she was a bird of ill omen. And toward her fellow-actresses she was as savage as a scorpion: for she was very malicious. . . . Thus was this woman born and bred, and her name was a byword beyond that of other common wenches on the tongues of all men.

. . . Justinian fell violently in love with her. At first he kept her only as a mistress, though he raised her to patrician rank. Through him Theodora was able immediately to acquire an unholy power and exceedingly great riches. For she seemed to him the sweetest thing in the world, and like all lovers, he desired to please his charmer with every possible favor and requite her with all his wealth. . . . With her now to help spend his money he plundered the people more than ever, not only in the capital, but throughout the entire Roman Empire. . . .

Now as long as the former Empress was alive, Justinian was unable to find a way to make Theodora his wedded wife. In this one matter [the Empress] opposed him as in nothing else; for the lady abhorred vice. . . . But finally her death removed this obstacle to Justinian's desire. . . .

It was then that he undertook to complete his marriage with Theodora. But as it was impossible for a man of senatorial rank to make a courtesan his wife, this being forbidden by ancient law, he made the Emperor [Justinian's aged uncle was still Emperor at this time] nullify this ordinance by creating a new one, permitting him to wed Theodora, and consequently making it possible for anyone else to marry a courtesan. Immediately after this he seized the power of the Emperor. . . .

So Justinian and Theodora ascended the imperial throne three days before Easter, a time, indeed, when even making visits or greeting one's friends is forbidden. . . .

Thus it was that Theodora, though born and brought up as I have related, rose to royal dignity over all obstacles.

Whatever may be left of the Great Palace of the Byzantine emperors now lies under the mosques and busy streets of present-day Istanbul. But excavations in recent years have uncovered part of the foundations and some vivid mosaics in what was a courtyard of one of the palace buildings. The young woman carrying a water jug on her shoulder and the two boys being led around on a camel are details from this pavement, which was probably laid down between A.D. 450 and 550.

Justinian, it was eventually to be recognized as the crowning glory of the Empire.

Constantine also set up a huge column—ten drums of porphyry, bound in metal—rising from a white marble plinth and supporting a Greek Apollo whose head was replaced by that of the Emperor encircled with the golden rays of the sun. Within the plinth were enshrined such purported relics of special veneration as a casket holding crumbs from the bread with which Christ fed the five thousand, the adze with which Noah built the ark, the alabaster box of ointment with which Mary anointed Jesus, and the crosses of the two thieves crucified with Jesus of Nazareth which the Emperor's mother, Saint Helena of York, had recently brought from Jerusalem. The inscription on the plinth of Constantine's column read: "O Christ, Ruler and Master of the World, to Thee have I now consecrated this obedient City. . . ." On May 11, A.D. 330, the city was solemnly dedicated and the Byzantine Empire inaugurated.

For this empire Constantine the Great laid both the temporal and spiritual foundations, and in it he fused together the great political legacy of Rome, the equally great cultural legacy of the Hellenic world, and the explosive dynamism of the Christian faith. It was to last for 1,123 years, and to be governed by no less than eighty-eight effective rulers in succession.

For convenience this long period can be divided into phases. The first—from the foundation of Constantinople in 330 to the death of the emperor Anastasius in 518—was one of growth and trial. Thanks partly to its geographical position, the new city escaped the barbarian devastations that visited the West. Only in one battle, at Adrianople in 378, were the armies of the Eastern Empire defeated by the Goths; and it may in part have been the recollection of this defeat that prompted Cyrus, prefect of the emperor Theodosius II, to build a huge triple line of walls to the landward side of the seagirt promontory on which Constantinople stands. The impressive ruins of these walls may still be seen.

The second phase, from 518 to 610, or from Justin I to Phocas, is marked above all by the reign of the emperor Justinian and his wife Theodora. Fired by an ambition to bring within the orbit of Byzantium all those alienated lands of the old Roman Empire, and to establish his imperial government over the whole of the Mediterranean and Western world, Justinian embarked on a policy of territorial aggrandizement which strained the resources of the Empire to their limits. In twenty years (533–554), he brought northern Africa, Italy, southern Spain, and the islands of Sicily, Corsica, Sardinia, and the Balearics under Byzantine rule. At the same time he initiated a series of internal reforms. In spite of the wealth and splendor of the imperial capital, the whole administrative machinery was in urgent need of overhaul, and so great was popular discontent over the

various abuses that in 532 a revolt, known as the Nika riot, broke out at Constantinople and all but cost Justinian his throne. That it did not was due to the courage of Theodora and, it must be added, to the loyalty and brutality of the imperial guards who, after half the original city of Constantinople had been burned to the ground, put down the revolt by slaughtering some thirty thousand of the insurgents in the Hippodrome.

Justinian, in order to remove the causes of the riot, set about at once to centralize the administration, abolishing the sale of offices and tightening up provincial government. But his greatest work, already begun in the opening years of his reign, was the recodification of Roman law. In a series of volumes, collectively known as the *Codex Justinianus,* the primary rules of social existence as defined by Roman law were reformulated in accordance with the Christian ethic. It became the civil code not only of Byzantium but of much of the Western world in subsequent centuries. Finally, Justinian set about repairing the damage caused to the capital by the fires of the Nika riot. Various new civic buildings were erected, and a bronze equestrian statue of the Emperor himself, wearing what was referred to as the armor of

Achilles, was set up on a huge column in the main public square, the Augustaeum. Above all, the great church of Constantinople, Hagia Sophia, had to be reconstructed. In five years and ten months the two major architects, Isidore the Milesian and Anthemius of Tralles, raised a building that was to be forever after the pride and pivot of the Byzantine world, a visible expression of the vital consciousness—compounded of Roman, Greek, and Christian elements—of the Byzantine people.

*F*or behind the pageant of the eleven-hundred-odd years of their history lies a deliberate and unchanging pattern, a particular vision of human life and its purposes that gives an underlying unity to the shifting scenes of the historical drama. Byzantium was above all a Christian empire; before we can understand its unique nature, we must try to discern what meaning and relevance this fact had for the Byzantines themselves. Here we may have recourse to the image of the dome. Set over all, seeming to contain and embrace in its simple unity all the diversity and multitude that lies below it, the dome is the Byzantine architectural form par excellence. And the dome of all Byzantine domes was that of

PHOTO YAN: LEFT: MARTIN HURLIMANN—VIKING PRESS, N.Y.; THAMES & HUDSON, LONDON

The focus of public life in Constanti-
nople was the Hippodrome (right),
where the screech of chariot wheels and
the snarls of wild beasts competed with
the screams of the "Blue" and "Green"
factions (everyone was passionately com-
mitted to one or the other) as they made
and unmade heroes—and emperors. The
arena, with its races, circuses, fights, and
shows, was the one place where the peo-
ple could express their feelings, very
often in the presence of the emperor him-
self. The relief above, showing the em-
peror Theodosius and his family in the
royal box, is on the base of the farther
obelisk—which came originally from the
Temple of Karnak in Egypt and was
erected on the long axis of the Hippo-
drome in A.D. *390. The masonry shaft in*
the foreground is the Walled Obelisk, or
Column of Constantine Porphyrogenitus.
Between the two, in a circular pit (the
ground level has since risen) is the low
Serpentine Column brought from Delphi
by Constantine the Great. The four
bronze horses opposite once graced the
Hippodrome, too; but the Venetians car-
ried them off in 1204, and they now
prance above the portal of St. Mark's.

13

14

The minor arts of Byzantium are notable for their richness of detail, sumptuous materials, and sophisticated craftsmanship. The two examples shown here both date from the sixth century A.D. At the right is a reliquary cross of silver gilt (the gold base is a later addition) sent to the Vatican by the emperor Justin II. It encloses a piece of the True Cross and is still carried in Good Friday processions in St. Peter's basilica. The elaborately carved plaque opposite is part of the so-called Barberini ivory and shows the Emperor as Champion of the Faith—but which emperor? History seems to support Anastasius, who received an embassy from India in 496. The small figures at bottom right are bringing him gifts of ivory, an elephant, and a tiger.

Hagia Sophia—a dome so light, as the contemporary historian Procopius wrote, that it "does not appear to rest upon a solid foundation, but to cover the place beneath as though it were suspended from heaven by the fabled golden chain."

This description is not merely figurative; nor is that other sixth-century witness, Paul the Silentiary, being merely figurative when he calls the dome a "great helmet, which bending over like the radiant heavens embraces the church." The language is one of an intelligible symbolism; to recall the egglike helmets of the Dioscuri, Castor and Pollux, and to learn that those two pagan heroes, gods of the tomb and intermediaries between heaven and earth, had a place in the Christian imagination of Byzantium, is to understand what the poet meant when he referred to the dome as a helmet. It was the desire to make visible a certain complex of ideas, and not any structural or utilitarian interest in a means of covering space, that impelled the emperor Justinian and the subsequent builders of Byzantine architecture to give such prominence to the dome and to the building of domed churches and palaces. It was wholly natural that the visitor who approached the holy city of Constantinople from across the dolphin-torn silvery blue of the Sea of Marmara, and rounded the promontory to enter the Golden Horn, saw rising on the spacious platform of the headland—over the masts of the merchantmen and the roofs of the warehouses, over the Hippodrome and the Senate House and the Great Imperial Palace, over the public square of the Augustaeum

with its armor-clad statue of the Emperor on his enormous column—the huge domed mass of Hagia Sophia.

For this church expressed that consciousness of a transcendent reality, of a supernatural presence, which lay at the heart of Byzantine life. It was a replica of heaven upon earth, of Paradise, of the house of God. And the crowning glory of the church was the dome, invested with a symbolism both divine and royal. It is enough to recall that the Achaemenid kings of Persia, who gave the classical world its conception of a divine and universal ruler, used to hold court under a dome (though the dome of a tent); and that Alexander the Great, in imitation of them, made his appearances, according to Plutarch, in "a magnificent tent made with fifty gilded posts which carried a sky of rich workman-

TEXT CONTINUED ON PAGE 20

OVERLEAF: The most famous surviving Byzantine mosaics are not in ravaged Constantinople but in Ravenna, which from the sixth to the eighth century was the Byzantine capital in the West. The two reproduced here are ceremonial portraits of Justinian and Theodora in the Church of San Vitale, which was built under their patronage. The Emperor (no doubt an excellent likeness) is carrying a votive offering and accompanied by clergy and members of his retinue. In the stiffly regal portrait of Theodora that follows there is little to suggest her beginnings as the daughter of a bearkeeper in the Hippodrome and as the sixth-century equivalent of a show girl.

15

The original exterior of Hagia Sophia is buried today under a lumpish mass of buttresses, minarets, and other accretions. But the interior, over which the great dome seems to float, is still—despite the grime of centuries, the loss of many decorations, and the distracting medallions of Arabic script—one of the most majestic and moving sights in the Western world. Although in continuous use for almost fourteen hundred years as a place of prayer, it is today neither church nor mosque: in 1935 it was secularized and made a museum.

TEXT CONTINUED FROM PAGE 15

ship"; and that from this derived the jeweled and golden baldachin in which the Byzantine emperor in his turn appeared in state as the supreme earthly ruler, vice-regent and vicegerent of God. This half-divine, half-royal symbolism was transferred to the dome of the Christian church, and was there linked with the majesty of Christ. It was his image, as Christ Pantocrator, the All-Ruler, that animated the space of the dome. Situated at the central point of the earthly and heavenly kingdom, scene of the manifestation of the Christian Saviour, the dome was thus a symbol of transcendent power and authority as well as of the Resurrection and the coming of the Kingdom of God in which human life and society would be fulfilled. In it were thus embodied the multiple ideals and purposes which gave Byzantium its *raison d'être* and which the Empire, in theory at least, was consciously intended to realize.

*H*ence the importance the architectural form of the dome assumes in Byzantium. It was Christ—*"Christos Basileus"* —who was the true founder, ruler, and consummation of the God-supported and God-protected Christian empire of Byzantium. It was his law, as manifest in the Gospels, that was to provide the pattern for imperial life; his Cross was carried at the front of military processions; his image, crowned with the imperial diadem, was stamped on coins; it was in his name, "The Lord Jesus Christ, our Master," that laws were promulgated.

But if Christ was the spiritual ruler of Byzantium, his temporal instrument for achieving the corporate salvation of his chosen nation was the Christian emperor. Although formally elected by the Senate and proclaimed by the people and the army, the emperor was in fact regarded as chosen by divine decree and therefore as occupying a position superior to that of other mortals. "Glory to God who has designated you as basileus, who has glorified you, who has manifested His grace to you" ran the acclamation which followed the imperial coronation. Temporal representative of Christ, the emperor was equal to the Apostles, *isapostolos*; and the mystical procession of his days as well as the elaborations of court ceremonial were patterned on the example of his celestial paradigm. His costume was like an icon. At Easter he donned the garb of resurrection, and appeared surrounded by twelve apostles, his body swathed in white bands. Twelve guests sat at his table at meals. His receptions were not so much audiences as epiphanies, divine appearances. In the Sacred Palace they took place in an octagonal room crowned with an immense cupola and furnished with glittering chandeliers, golden lions, golden griffins, golden birds perched on golden branches, the birds breaking into song when some mysterious device was set in motion. At the heart of all this, on the imperial throne, was the sovereign himself, clothed in gold, bathed in sanctity. Sacred, too, was all he touched—his garments, his letters, the golden imperial seal. To insult him was to blaspheme. To revolt against his

For more than a hundred years, beginning in 726, the Empire was shaken by the great religious controversy over the worship of images, which gave to later ages the useful word "iconoclast." These events are recalled in the delicate illuminations below, from an eleventh-century Greek psalter. At the top are two pro-icon Church fathers supporting an image; at the bottom they are shown remonstrating with Emperor Leo V while his iconoclast followers deface an image with lime. When the worship of icons was restored in 843, sacred art flourished anew to produce such great works as the mosaic opposite, which is in the narthex of Hagia Sophia. It probably portrays Leo VI, called the Wise, in an attitude of complete spiritual submission to Christ, who here embodies Holy Wisdom.

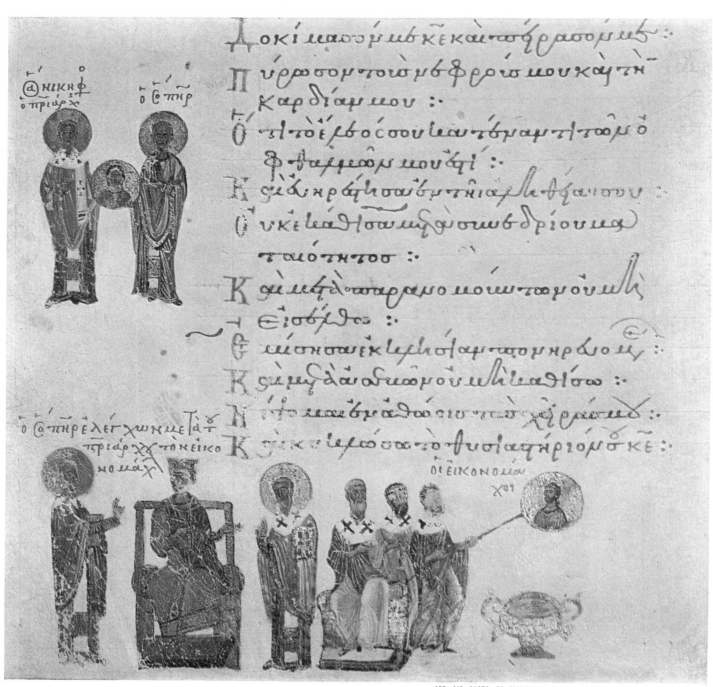

22

authority was to invite excommunication. Rebellion was apostasy. And this sanctity of the sovereign flowed over into that of his ministers, and indeed into the whole imperial administration. Entrance into public office was a kind of ordination; to leave it was to lay down a sacred trust. The veneration due to the emperor in this way conferred on the whole imperial service a truly hieratic character.

Indeed this civil service—massive and proficient, inherited directly from Rome—was the backbone of the state. Down to Justinian's day it used Latin as its official language and preserved Latin titles for its senior officials (Praetorian Prefect, Magister Militum, Quaestor Sacri Palatii, and so on). But from the seventh century onward the service gradually assumed a new form. Greek became the official language. Greek designations replaced the Latin titles of ministers and high officials. Of these the most numerous were the logothetes, ministers of internal and foreign affairs, of public revenues and imperial estates, and of the military chest. Generally, though not necessarily, these great functionaries were recruited, after passing a stiff examination, from distinguished families with a tradition of public service. They were nominated, promoted, and dismissed by the emperor; it was he who conferred upon them the emblems of office, and it was with him that the actuality of power lay. No parliament or senate encumbered the emperor in his dealings with his officials or stultified the everyday working of

the state machine. The same was true where provincial administration was concerned: each province was ruled by a general, or strategos, directly appointed by the emperor and directly responsible to him. At the same time, as a check against the abuse of power on the part of the military governor and the growth of local despotisms, a representative of the civil interest was appointed alongside him, though in a subordinate position; and he, too, was in direct communication with the emperor. This combination of highly trained officials and military aristocrats all personally known to, chosen by, and directly responsible to the emperor, made the Byzantine administration one of the most centralized and at the same time one of the most efficient of which we have a record.

*I*f the regulation and administration of the material and temporal side of life lay with the emperor and his service, the spiritual and eternal side of life was most fully represented not by the bishops and clergy, as might be imagined, but by the monasteries and hermitages. It is impossible to overestimate the significance of the role played by monasticism in Byzantium. It was not simply that monasteries were places in which deposed emperor and downtrodden peasant alike could find refuge—a kind of safety valve through which rejected or disruptive elements might be discharged without the system exploding. It was that the mon-

Above: One explanation, not entirely facetious, for the long persistence of the Byzantine Empire was its possession of a secret weapon, "Greek fire." The exact composition is not known; but it apparently included naphtha, sulphur, and saltpeter, and its use anticipated the modern flame thrower. A fourteenth-century manuscript of the chronicles of John Skylitzes shows it being directed against a boatload of troops.

Below: Another illustration from the Skylitzes manuscript is captioned "The Romans chase, the Russians flee" (the Byzantines called themselves Romans). The two empires were often in direct competition in the Balkans. On this occasion, in the tenth century, the Russians had demanded that the Byzantines withdraw to Asia and leave them Constantinople—a dream that has haunted the Russian mind ever since.

asteries, and more particularly the craggy fastness or desert cave of the hermits, were the forging-houses of what the Byzantines regarded as the highest types of humanity, the types in which the Christian ideal was realized to the fullest possible extent on earth. The emperor might be God's elect. The saint or the holy man was more: he was a living holocaust of divine energies, the incarnation of the Holy Spirit, witness of God, and in a certain sense God himself. For the Byzantines saw the highest type of humanity fulfilled not in those who lived a terrestrial life of moral rectitude or judicious piety, but in those who through earnest battle had broken the barrier between man and God, and had fused the two once more into a vital conjunction. It was this union that the saint or the holy man had accomplished.

The saint or the holy man was a mediator between earth and heaven. He was a present source of mercy, miracle, and guidance, the father of the people among whom he dwelt, their healer and deliverer. Mortal life was a constant warfare between myriad unseen forces, divine and demoniac, ever-present, overwhelming, unappeasable. Where else could a man turn but to those who through divine power could subject even the demons to their bidding? Let disease or other affliction come, the holy man was at hand with his healing grace. Let taxgatherer extort or landowner oppress, the ascetic saint was there to defend against the rapine and injustice of the powerful. Let the emperor himself, out of considerations of state, seek to impose some dogma contrary to the faith and, weather-wracked and gaunt, the man of God would descend from pillar or mountain retreat to head the opposition that brought the erring sovereign to heel. For what had the ascetic to fear at the hands of the powerful, even if they were the hands of the emperor himself? He had already renounced the world and all its ways. All that could be taken from him now was his mortal life, and if he were to lose that through violence laid upon him, it might well be but to gain a martyr's crown and so to become an even stronger focal point of popular worship and superhuman aid than he already was. Fanatic to us though they may often appear, the fact remains that throughout the Byzantine period it was from their ranks—the ranks of the monks and the nuns—that came those heroic men and women who guarded the Empire's conscience, its spiritual lifeblood. Through them the springs of its inspiration flowed and, barren though it may seem to say it in an age of disbelief, to them was Byzantium chiefly indebted for all that was most vital in her achievement.

Between the material and the temporal, represented in Byzantium by the emperor and the imperial body politic, and the spiritual and the eternal, represented by the saints, there is the image-forming world of the soul, the world of the imagination. It is the world of Byzantine art, which not only gave expression to the divine and supernatural aspirations of man, but also to those transcendental realities which are the objects of his spiritual quest. Its sources and intent therefore coincided with those of Christianity itself, and like other forms of Christian worship its chief function was to serve the religion to which it owed its existence. The forms and figures of Byzantine art reflect that necessity. The symbolism is intelligible, clear, subtle, allowing for the intrusion of no pleasing sentiment or vacant naturalism. All is simplified, all reduced to essentials, all subordinate to the spiritual truth which is being conveyed. To this sparse geometry of symbolic content, color gave the flesh, color employed not merely as an adjunct to the modeling but fired with an independent life. But one must also remark the subtlety of contour, the impeccable sense of proportion, the superb grasp of the whole that brought all the elaborate detail into harmony with the overriding symbolic pattern; and finally the unbridled richness of material employed—stones, metals, fabrics, marbles, and mosaic. Having absorbed all this, one may understand something of the magnificence of this art, and of its sophisticated splendor.

*T*he first flowering of Byzantine art begins with the foundation of Constantinople in A.D. 330 and reaches its golden age under Justinian in the sixth century. This period coincided with the final decadence of Hellenistic art, which had spread across the Mediterranean and Anatolian world from Rome to Bactria—unrooted, cosmopolitan, dominated by the natural world and with the natural human form as its final measure and norm. Already in the Near East the revival of Persia and the foundation of the Sasanian empire in A.D. 226 had brought a reaction and a return to a more hieratic convention. Byzantine art may be seen as the result of the imposition of Oriental forms on a Hellenistic ground. In it an almost preternatural insight into the significance of intelligible forms is fused with a lyrical sensuality that prevents stylization from becoming academic and lifeless, the mere repetition of formulas. This fusion, still incomplete in the famous Ravenna mosaics (see pages 16–19), seems nonetheless to have been achieved in Justinian's reign, if one is to judge from the astonishing mosaics recently restored to their full brilliance in the apse of the Church of Saint Catherine on Mount Sinai. At the same time there came about the architectural fusion of the early Christian basilica (square atrium or narthex, rounded apse, and long naves flanked by twin or quadruple rows of pillars) with the domed octagon or rotunda—a fusion crystallized in Justinian's new church of Hagia Sophia. "Solomon, I have surpassed thee," Justinian is reported to have said when first he viewed the immense majesty of the completed edifice; and he celebrated its dedication with a banquet at which six thousand sheep, a thousand each of oxen, pigs, and poultry, and half a thousand deer were roasted for the delectation of court and populace alike.

This church remains, even as the secularized museum it is today, Justinian's most enduring monument. His attempt to reconstitute the Roman Empire proved politically a great burden; and the ensuing phase of Byzantine history, opening with the reign of Heraclius in 610 and ending with that of Theodosius III in 717, was one in which the existence of the whole Empire was imperiled. First came the onslaughts of the Persian armies under Khosrau II in the East, followed by the attacks of the Avars and the Lombards in the West. Then, in 634, within three years after the death of Mohammed, his Arab followers from Medina attacked the Byzantine garrisons of Palestine. By 640, Palestine was lost and Egypt invaded; by 641, the year Heraclius died, Alexandria was evacuated and Persia and Armenia were overrun. Cyprus fell, and in 655 the Byzantine fleet, under the emperor Constans II, was defeated off the coast of Lycia. But largely as a result of the discovery and effective use of a new weapon, Greek fire, the Moslems were finally brought to a halt on both land and sea, and in 678 peace was concluded. Much reduced in size, the Byzantine Empire was from then on centered on Constantinople and the Greek seaboard, while connections with the West grew correspondingly weaker; it was at this time, for instance, that the last vestiges of Latin were dropped from official imperial usage.

*T*he fourth phase, from 717 to 867, began with a restoration of the prestige of Byzantine arms under the Isaurian emperors Leo and Constantine V Copronymus. The Moslems attacked again and laid siege to Constantinople itself, but the Byzantines, with the considerable aid of frost and famine, inflicted a loss of some one hundred fifty thousand men on the besiegers. That defeat stemmed for a time the tide of Arab expansion: the capital of the Abbasid caliphs was now transferred to the distant city of Baghdad.

But the great event of this phase of Byzantine history lay not in the field of military triumph or of internal reform, but in that of religion. The worship of sacred images, or icons, had by this time become an integral part of Orthodox Christianity. And thus when the emperor Leo, supported by his puritanical followers from the hinterland of Asia Minor, launched an attack on image worship in an edict of 726, reaction was immediate and intense. Riots in the capital were soon followed by insurrection in Greece, Byzantine authority in Italy was fatally undermined, and the whole Empire was split asunder. Even the restoration of the worship of images by the empress Irene in 787 did not bring an end to the troubles. In 815, with the advent of a new emperor from Armenia, icons were once again proscribed; and

The rape of Constantinople by the Fourth Crusade in 1204 is the subject of this splendidly romantic canvas by the nineteenth-century French painter Eugène Delacroix. The central figure is Baldwin of Flanders, commander of the French contingent. About the fall of the city one Byzantine wrote: "Even the Saracens are merciful and kind" when compared to those "who bear the cross of Christ upon their shoulders."

it was only because most orthodox Christians, and particularly the monks, remained so intransigent in their attachment to sacred pictures that the iconoclasts, or "image-breakers," were finally defeated.

The restoration of images after these struggles ushers in a new period of Byzantine art, which continues through the eleventh and twelfth centuries. It is a period marked by the huge patronage of such emperors as Basil I the Macedonian, whose reconquest of imperial territories at the end of the ninth century launched the Empire's most prosperous times; Constantine VII Porphyrogenitus, who as a patron of the arts has been compared to Hadrian and Lorenzo the Magnificent; and Alexius I Comnenus, whose life and character were recorded so graphically by his daughter Anna. This was the period of Byzantine culture's widest diffusion. Of the profane art of the time, such as that which decorated the Great Palace at Constantinople, little or nothing remains, and our notion of it must be derived chiefly from contemporary chronicles. But of ecclesiastical art, refined and spiritualized after the attacks of the iconoclasts, memorials exist as far apart geographically as the mosaics in Santa Sophia at Kiev and the enthroned Christ at Monreale in Sicily; lying between them, in Greece, are such masterpieces as the monastery churches of Daphne, near Athens, Saint Luke in Phocis, and Nea Moni on the island of Chios.

A single dynasty, that of the Macedonians, fills the two hundred years between 867 and 1057. It was a period of territorial expansion and internal prosperity, in which the forces of Islam were thrust back to the deserts of Arabia and the hills of Kurdistan, while many of the lost provinces and cities of the East were reclaimed. In 961 the capture of Crete restored control of the Aegean to the Byzantine navy, and by 1014 the emperor Basil II Bulgaroctonos (the Bulgar-slayer) had reduced the whole Balkan Peninsula to imperial rule. External success was marked by a corresponding prodigality at home. All the world's wealth seemed to pour through the trade routes of the Levant, overland from India and beyond, or down the great Russian rivers and the Black Sea into the queen of cities, there to furnish fresh magnificence in art and architecture. The only signs of trouble to come were the increasing independence of the great feudal overlords; the growing alienation of the West, soon to lead to official schism with Rome; and the deepening shadow of the Seljuk Turks converging on the northeast frontiers.

Between 1053 and the sack of Constantinople by the Fourth Crusaders in 1204 these threats materialized. With the death of the last ruler of the Macedonian house in 1053 a thirty-year struggle for the possession of the throne broke out among the great feudal families, only resolved by the accession, in 1081, of Alexius I Comnenus, succeeded in turn by his son and grandson. Meanwhile the Seljuk Turks were continuing to expand, and in 1071 they routed the Byzantine armies at Manzikert, near Lake Van in eastern Anatolia,

The Glories of Kariye Çami

PHOTO YAN

The final flowering of Byzantine culture came after the expulsion of the Latins from Constantinople in 1261 under the Palaeologi emperors. In a remote corner of the city the church of the Chora—which became the Kariye Çami mosque (above)—remains the finest example of this last renaissance. The work of restoring the church's mosaics—such as the one opposite, portraying Theodore Metochites—has been the continuing project of the Byzantine Institute of America in Washington, D.C. A wealthy scholar, scientist, and imperial adviser, Metochites financed the repair of the Chora between 1310–1320 to assure—as he wrote—the salvation of his soul and the immortality of his memory. Besides new wings, he added a library of precious manuscripts and adorned it with rare marbles and mosaics. The inscription proclaims him as builder and Grand Logothete (administrator) of the Treasury. The model he is holding shows the church as it was before the Turks converted it into a mosque.

taking the emperor Romanus IV Diogenes prisoner. This defeat was the prelude to the loss of the greater part of Byzantine territory in Asia Minor. Six years after Manzikert the Turks occupied Jerusalem, and their possession of the holy places there both incited the chivalry and tempted the land hunger of the West. The First Crusade was launched by the Council of Clermont in 1095. Already relationships between the Orthodox Christian churches and the church at Rome had been strained beyond the breaking point, and a state of open schism had been proclaimed and ratified by Patriarch and Pope alike. Hence, to the crusaders the Greeks of Byzantium were neither Christians nor brothers, and were in fact scarcely less legitimate objects for their ill-disciplined and rapacious armies than the Moslems themselves. The Second Crusade in 1147, led by the emperor Conrad Hohenstaufen and King Louis VII of France, looted and raped its way through Byzantine lands till its final defeat by the Turks. In the Third Crusade of 1189 a Norman-Sicilian fleet sacked Salonika with particular brutality. But it was with the Fourth Crusade that the full depredation of the Western host broke over the Byzantines: in 1204 the Latins assaulted and took Constantinople, the virgin city was handed over to wholesale plunder, and the accumulated treasures of nearly nine centuries, including those works of classical art which Constantine the Great had brought to his capital, were committed to destruction. It is one of the ironies of history that it was the soldiers of the Cross who were responsible for the rape of the queen of Christian cities and that it was they who prepared the way for the overthrow of the Christian empire.

During the Latin occupation of Constantinople the Byzantine capital was transferred to Nicaea in Asia Minor, and the next-to-last phase of Byzantine history covers the fifty-seven years of exile. In the European territories of the Empire a series of petty semifeudal dependencies, of which the most important were the kingdom of Thessalonica under Boniface of Montferrat, the barony of Athens, and the principality of Achaia, were set up in vassalage to Baldwin of Flanders, Latin emperor-elect in Constantinople. But this attempt of Western chivalry to take over the Empire proved as abortive as it was misconceived. Within a year Baldwin and Boniface were at war with each other, and both were killed before three years were out. Henry of Flanders, Baldwin's brother, survived only till 1216, to be succeeded by the children of his sister, Yelande. Of these the youngest, Baldwin II, came to the throne at the age of eleven in 1228, and reigned until Michael VIII Palaeologus—concluding a treaty with the Genoese which granted them, in return for naval assistance, the privileges held by the Venetians in Greek lands—crossed from Nicaea to Europe and in 1261 recaptured Constantinople. Baldwin II, the Latin Patriarch, and the Venetians fled.

And so the Byzantine Empire, diminished but still vigorous, entered upon the final phase of its history, under the dynasty of the Palaeologi. The period was one of gallant rear-guard actions against overwhelming odds. The Empire itself was confined to Nicaea and the northwest corner of Asia Minor, Constantinople and Thrace, Salonika and part of Macedonia, and a few islands. The capital had been devastated and deserted; the working of the administrative machinery had been disrupted; Italians monopolized the trade; Bulgars, Serbs, and above all the Turks menaced every frontier; and still another crusade against the Greeks threatened from the West. After the death of Michael VIII in 1282, civil war over the succession further weakened the state. Meanwhile, the Turks were gradually advancing. By 1345 they had crossed from Asia Minor to Europe. Soon they had overrun the whole Balkan Peninsula, and it was only their defeat by the Tartar army of Tamerlane in 1402 that prevented them from taking Constantinople itself. Even so, the respite was short. Some twenty years later the Turks had entered Albania and the Peloponnesus. Salonika was captured in 1430. In a last desperate attempt to secure help from the West, the emperor John VIII Palaeologus tried to persuade his bishops to cede to the demands of the Roman Church. Union between the Orthodox and Latin churches was actually celebrated at Florence in 1439. But it proved an empty formality: at Constantinople neither monks, clergy, nor people accepted the decision, and in any case the Western forces sent to assist the Byzantines were defeated at Varna on the Black Sea in 1444. Still the Byzantines behind the walls of Constantinople held out. But in 1451 Mohammed II became the leader of the Ottoman Turks: the last years had come.

The sense of impending doom was vivid throughout this final period under the Palaeologi emperors, and yet it saw a renaissance of the arts of which the paintings at Mistra in the Peloponnesus and the decorations of many churches in Constantinople itself, especially of Kariye Çami (pages 28–30), allow us to gauge the mastery. Even if weakened by the naturalism that later reduced art in Italy to the level of sensa-

"The cannons decided the whole issue," wrote the Greek Critobulus of the attack on Constantinople by the Ottoman Turks. In April, 1453, Sultan Mohammed II assembled an army of 150,000 before the city's landward walls and aimed his heavy artillery—here used in the East for the first time—directly at its heart. As portrayed in a contemporary French miniature, janissaries and brightly costumed viziers mill about the Sultan's gold silk tent. To gain access to the Golden Horn, barred from the Bosporus by an impregnable bridge (top center), Turkish ships were hauled overland (upper left) around the fortified Genoese settlement of Galata. Within the city proper is Hagia Sophia, which the artist has imagined in the shape of a Gothic French cathedral. After fifty-three days of siege, Constantinople fell—and with it, the eleven-hundred-year-old Byzantine Empire.

tion, the hieratic form of these works still reflects the vigor and audacity of the Byzantine spiritual intellect, sharpened as this had been by recent controversies with theologians of the Latin West. If one needed to demonstrate the fact that the Byzantines, far from being moribund, effete, the hidebound victims of a religio-political system of their own making, retained their creative vitality even after a thousand years and more of historical existence, then the art and intellectual activity of this final period are there to supply the needed evidence.

The persistence of the classical tradition through the whole Byzantine period has already been indicated; and it may be added that if the Byzantines were not humanists, in that they did not regard man and his reason as the measure of reality, yet the study of the humanities was, except for a short period during the iconoclast struggles, an indispensable part of their intellectual training. Of music it is impossible to estimate the full richness: ecclesiastical music has survived in numerous manuscripts, but interpretation is difficult and uncertain. It seems safe to say, however, that the chants were akin to the Gregorian, which may in fact have derived from them. Literature, like the music and painting, was largely in the service of the Church, and reflected the same spiritual qualities. In the major theological works are enshrined the meditations of some of the most profound doctrinal masters of the Christian tradition, while the vast body of liturgical writings—hymns, prayers, and offices—combines theological penetration with rich lyrical imagery in a manner that is both dignified and immensely moving. Of secular poetry little is left, apart from a handful of epigrams such as those by Paul the Silentiary and Agathias which adorn several pages of the Greek Anthology; though there is that unique product of medieval Greek literature, the epic of Digenes Akritas, in which chivalresque adventure, Persian romance, and mythological imagery are expressed in a language reflecting the rhythms and strength of popular speech. The products of craftsmanship, in reliquaries of jewelers and goldsmiths' work, in glass, enamels, ivories, and fabrics, and in such other minor arts as the illumination of manuscripts —these emphasize on a smaller scale what architecture, painting, and literature demonstrate on a larger one, that the Byzantines were among the world's most perfect artificers.

One thing yet should be mentioned, and that is the role of Byzantium in the growth of Western civilization. For not only were the borders of Byzantium for the greater part of her historical existence more or less coterminous with those of Western civilization itself; but by the time of her overthrow in 1453 she had already planted seeds from which were to grow some of the major developments of modern Europe. Perhaps the two most important concern Italy and Russia; in any case they will suffice to indicate the magnitude of the Byzantine legacy. Where Italy is concerned, the old theory

A Poet's Byzantium

"I think if I could be given a month of Antiquity and leave to spend it where I chose, I would spend it in Byzantium a little before Justinian opened St. Sophia and closed the Academy of Plato. I think I could find in some little wine-shop some philosophical worker in mosaic who could answer all my questions, the supernatural descending nearer to him than to Plotinus even, for the pride of his delicate skill would make what was an instrument of power to princes and clerics, a murderous madness in the mob, show as a lovely flexible presence like that of a perfect human body.

"I think that in early Byzantium, maybe never before or since in recorded history, religious, aesthetic and practical life were one, that architect and artificers . . . spoke to the multitude and the few alike. The painter, the mosaic worker, the worker in gold and silver, the illuminator of sacred books, were almost impersonal, almost perhaps without the consciousness of individual design, absorbed in their subject matter and that the vision of a whole people. They could copy out of old Gospel books those pictures that seemed as sacred as the text, and yet weave all into a vast design, the work of many that seemed the work of one, that made building, picture, pattern, metal-work of rail and lamp, seem but a single image. . . ."

—William Butler Yeats, from *A Vision*, 1925

*. . . And therefore I have sailed the seas and come
To the holy city of Byzantium.*

*O sages standing in God's holy fire
As in the gold mosaic of a wall,
Come from the holy fire, pern in a gyre,*
And be the singing-masters of my soul.
Consume my heart away; sick with desire
And fastened to a dying animal
It knows not what it is; and gather me
Into the artifice of eternity.*

*Once out of nature I shall never take
My bodily form from any natural thing,
But such a form as Grecian goldsmiths make
Of hammered gold and gold enamelling
To keep a drowsy Emperor awake;
Or set upon a golden bough to sing
To lords and ladies of Byzantium
Of what is past, or passing, or to come.*

—W. B. Yeats, from "Sailing to Byzantium," 1927

* a hawk wheeling in a circle

that the fall of Constantinople loosed a flood of scholars and classical manuscripts upon the Italian world, and thus kindled the Renaissance, has long been discarded. Nonetheless, through those long centuries which separate the ancient Greco-Roman world from the Renaissance, the classical tradition—the literature and art of ancient Greece—was part of the living heritage of the Byzantine world, and it was through Byzantium that it was transmitted to Renaissance Italy and hence to the whole of the modern Western world.

*W*here Russia is concerned, the direct influence of Byzantium is less through culture than through religion and imperial tradition. The conversion of Russia to Christianity was largely linked with the activities of Olga, daughter-in-law of Rurik, the founder of the Russian state, and of her grandson Vladimir. Olga visited Constantinople in order to "learn about God," and there she was baptized, with the emperor Constantine VII Porphyrogenitus as her godfather. Vladimir, after assisting the emperor Basil II Bulgaroctonos to put down a revolt, was given Basil's sister in marriage; thenceforth, from 989, Christianity became the official religion of the Russian state. The final seal of Byzantine influence on Russia was set when, in 1472, after the fall of Constantinople, Sophia Palaeologina, survivor of the Palaeologue dynasty, married Ivan III of Muscovy. It was she who introduced Byzantine court ceremonial into the Russian court; the Kremlin was built at Moscow in imitation of the Great Palace at Constantinople; and the Byzantine bureaucratic system, its titles and usages, and even the double-headed eagle and the designation "Autocrat," borne by the Byzantine emperors for eleven hundred years, were adopted by the Russian state. Not for nothing was Moscow to be known as the third and final Rome.

Its predecessor lasted for a little more than a millennium, and then the city of Constantine was invested by the Turks. Mohammed II brought his giant artillery into action; the final preparations for assault were made. Within the city the last Byzantine emperor, Constantine XI Dragases Palaeologus, remained with his people despite frequent appeals to escape. On the afternoon of May 28, 1453, a day of ill omen, the last Christian service was held in the great church of Hagia Sophia. Relics and icons were brought out. After the service, Emperor and Patriarch bade public farewell. Then all took their posts to await the attack. Before the dawn of May 29 it came. A breach was forced in the great walls and the Sultan's soldiery poured through. The Emperor, discarding the insignia of his office, plunged into the fighting and was killed on the ramparts. Constantinople fell, and with its fall the Byzantine Empire was at an end.

Philip Sherrard, Research Fellow of St. Anthony's College, Oxford, and Deputy Director of the British School of Archaeology, Athens, is author of The Greek East and the Latin West.

By ROBERT HATCH

TYRONE GUTHRIE: THE ARTIST AS MAN OF THE THEATRE

He goes about the world leaving monuments behind him—theatres, built around his faith in a repertory of classic drama. The latest, though the first actually bearing his name, opened this year in Minnesota

It is accurate to say that Sir Tyrone Guthrie is the most renowned and probably most controversial of contemporary British stage directors (in compliance with a venerable English theatre tradition he is of Irish stock); but this identification does not explain why last summer the much gratified and more than a little astonished citizens of Minneapolis discovered that their city had become, for a season, the most exciting theatre town in America. A superb new playhouse named for Guthrie had been built, a repertory company that combined magnetic stars with group versatility had been assembled, a season of four world-famous plays had been sumptuously mounted, and Minneapolis found itself playing theatre host not only to the Middle West but to pilgrims from every state of the Union and points abroad.

To understand how this happy and almost ludicrously unlikely bolt of drama hit the Middle West, it is necessary to describe Guthrie, not merely as a director (he could as well be a producer or an actor), but as a man of the theatre—using that term as one says man of letters, to designate someone who is concerned for the standards, creative vigor, and public recognition of the art to which he has dedicated his life.

As a young man, just after World War I, Guthrie seems to have recognized in himself unusual resources of creative energy; at any rate, he decided quite soberly to become a celebrated artist. He thought first of being a singer, but his voice, though large, was not entirely pleasing. He turned then to acting, but the stage does not offer a great variety of roles to a man six foot five and amply framed for his height. Radio had just been born and Guthrie, pending the arrival of fame, took a job with the Belfast station of the B.B.C. There, putting an occasional dramatic half-hour on the air, he found in himself a knack for making rehearsals "go with a swing." A gentleman from Scotland observed him one day exercising this talent and invited him to present himself to the board of the Scottish National Players. He got the job, though his new employers were not conspicuously gracious in bestowing it— they made clear their total inability to find anyone else.

Guthrie did not awake the next morning in Glasgow to find himself famous. Indeed, reading his autobiography today,* it is not possible to say just when fame caught him in its current; and the most probable reason is that all his life Guthrie has worked as much for the theatre as in it. You can see this in the choices he made—when he was far enough along to have a choice: he habitually elected to associate himself with institutions. True, he has worked in the West End and on Broadway; he knows the intoxication of a hit and the hangover of a flop; he has respect for the commercial theatre and harsh words for colleagues who find its calculations and vulgarities offensive to their talents. He has said that a director who cannot make a stab at "staging anything from *Hamlet* to strip tease does not know his job."

* *A Life in the Theatre* (McGraw-Hill, 1959)

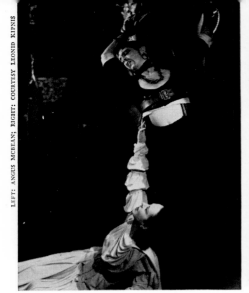

Sir Tyrone's staging always crackles with special effects which, in the hands of lesser directors, might seem extravagant. His range extends from Sophocles to a psychological drama he wrote himself, and in all he uses apt but unexpected devices. He fills up the height, as well as the breadth, of the proscenium, crowding acto onto balconies and surrounding them with eye-catching properties and settings.

Tense torsos in Jacobean melodrama:
John Webster's The White Devil

Greek tragedy played in masks:
Sophocles' Oedipus Rex

Nevertheless—from the National Players in Scotland, back to the B.B.C. in London, to the Festival Theatre in Cambridge, to the Canadian Broadcasting Company (as director of a serial called *The Romance of Canada,* sponsored by the Canadian National Railways), to a converted London movie house named the Westminster Theatre, to the Old Vic (where fame *did* catch up with him), to the Phoenix on Second Avenue in New York, to Habimah in Tel Aviv, to the Edinburgh International Festival, to the Festival Theatre in Stratford, Ontario, and now to the Tyrone Guthrie Theatre in Minneapolis—the mainstream of his career has been channeled into long-term organizations based on convictions rather than into short-term ventures based on risk capital. And in that world one is not "made" by a first night; fame does not rocket, it accumulates.

At any rate, Guthrie had become a celebrated figure by the end of World War II, and today his name is almost certain to head any popular list of "great" directors. The audience is aware of Guthrie, perhaps, because he is so very much aware of the audience. He likes it and understands it; he knows that it is a crowd and has pointed out that the way to a crowd is not through its mind but through its emotions.

Guthrie is also on record as deploring the pinch-mouthed view of the theatre that attempts to "elevate" it by pretend-ing that it is a school, a church, a political forum—it is, he insists, a place of entertainment. This is not frivolous, for Guthrie takes seriously the need for entertainment—recreation—in men's lives; but it is lighthearted and, together with his conviction that there can be no such thing as a definitive production of a great play, evokes a gusto, and daring enterprise on the stage, that the audience now recognizes as his mark.

His affinity for crowds, moreover, applies not only to the audience but to the stage itself: Guthrie is probably the most brilliant ensemble director of our era. Of course, every good director must be conscious of the broad stage picture, but Guthrie more than others seems to revel in the moments when the scene bursts out in flashing jewels and swirling capes, with trumpets sounding, armies passing, and fortune on the wing. Unlike most dramatic directors, he admires opera (but not its customary staging) and has mounted productions of *The Barber of Seville, Carmen, Falstaff,* and *La Traviata* at Sadler's Wells and the Metropolitan. He has staged every kind of play available to a modern director, from Ibsen to Sophocles, from J. B. Priestley to William Congreve, from *The Matchmaker* to *Tamburlaine,* but he will be remembered, I think, as the director who pounded the dust out of the classic spectacles and brought them roaring back to life. As the Canadian critic Robertson Davies has said: "What is realistic or small in scale is not for him; indeed, it does not easily survive his sort of treatment."

In the past ten or fifteen years the tangible evidence of Guthrie's activity is that wherever he applies himself you may expect to find that a new theatre of a particular design has been built and in it a company is playing a repertory of world classics. This was true at Edinburgh and at Stratford; last summer it became true at Minneapolis; and it is unlikely that the list will end there. As a man of the theatre Guthrie has developed a set of interlocking convictions, a philosophy, about the virtue and prosperity of his art; as a famous director he has a skill and a name to contribute to whatever enterprise will implement his convictions. Fame probably concerns him very little any more; he cannot, in any case, avoid it.

I would not give the impression that Guthrie is a latter-day Kubla Khan who goes about the world decreeing pleasure domes; a creation like the new theatre in Minneapolis rises from impulses much more complex than that. It began when two New York producers, Oliver Rea and Peter Zeisler, discovered that they were tired of the hit-and-run opportunism of Broadway and began to scan the country for some community that wanted a theatre rather than show business. They chose Minneapolis—or Minneap-

Romance on a balcony: Cyrano de Bergerac, *with Ralph Richardson*

Two levels for comedy: Twelfth Night *and Sir Toby's belch*

Height as a prop: Guthrie's own Top of the Ladder, *with John Mills and ladder*

olis chose them—because it was a rich town, a proud town, the site of the second largest university in America (Minnesota), and the gateway to one of the country's largest resort areas. And Guthrie, with whom Rea and Zeisler had baited their hook, liked Minneapolis—probably because it is the most American of cities and as far as you can possibly get from anything recognizable as organized theatre. If his theories worked there, they would work almost anywhere.

The Guthrie credo begins with the proposition that the essential magic of the theatre is not illusion but ritual. From this it follows that the classics are the plays in which men have found, not an imitation of life, but an occasion for the ceremonies that give life its shape and abstract its significance. And further it follows that the theatre in which such plays are to be mounted should provide a platform stage with the audience disposed in an encompassing arena —first, because the greatest of the classic playwrights, the Greeks and the Elizabethans, wrote for such a stage and second, because this design, in which the audience is aware of itself wrapped about the playing area, supporting, or as in French, "assisting at," the performance, most enhances the atmosphere of ritual. The commercial theatre can be relied upon to support a contemporary body of work (the unrecognized master-

piece is so rare as to be a myth), but it will not keep the classics alive. Therefore, a second, institutional theatre must be maintained, by subsidy if necessary. This should consist of repertory houses because repertory provides the richest public experience with the means available, and because it affords actors the variety of assignment and familiarity with the basic literature of their art without which they cannot become craftsmen. (Guthrie's most serious charges against the commercial theatre are that it offers the actors no goal beyond their own success and that it forces them either to jump rapidly from one failure to the next or to bury themselves for months, perhaps years, in a single role.)

That is Guthrie's credo; it is the program that was accepted at Minneapolis.

The theatre, adjoining the Walker Art Center and standing on land donated by that institution, has a frivolous exterior: a nonfunctional plywood molded screen of unconvincing abstract design which cost some $60,000—a sum that could have been better spent, I was somewhat bitterly informed by everyone in the company with whom I brought up the point, on backstage facilities and amenities. But the first impression is the only bad one: inside, the public spaces are large, functional, and relaxing; the auditorium, seating 1,437, is an arc sweeping 200 degrees around a platform stage of dark, lustrously polished wood. This

playing area is said to be a septagon, but when you are in the theatre its shape is inviting and elusive. Nothing in the Tyrone Guthrie auditorium is symmetrical. For two thirds of the arc, the rows of seats are arranged in orchestra and balcony, but very steeply raked; in the remaining third, the seats plunge uninterruptedly from ceiling to floor (the company calls this the ski jump, and club ladies have been seen to freeze when entering from above). The ceiling is baffled with a complex of acoustic "clouds," and the stage does not center upon any axis of the house. This ambiguity of design sets up a tension of expectancy in the audience; from the viewpoint of the productions, it makes relatively easy the creation of fluid stage patterns: the left-right, back-front *rigor mortis* that too often overcomes plays set within a proscenium is almost impossible on this enigmatic and versatile platform. At stage rear is a two-story "house" with windows and platforms, a functional structure in the Elizabethan pattern; it is mounted on two trucks and can be replaced by more specific "sets." Two broad ramps run from the stage under the audience; they allow almost instantaneous mobbing or evacuation of the stage.

The company, this first season, was headed by Hume Cronyn, his wife Jessica Tandy, George Grizzard, Rita Gam, and Zoe Caldwell. The assistant director, responsible for half the productions, was

Shakespeare's All's Well That
Ends Well *in 1914 British army uniforms*

Not Kiss Me, Kate *but* The Taming
of the Shrew *set, perhaps, in Oklahoma*

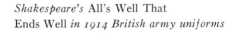

Douglas Campbell; Tanya Moiseiwitsch was the principal designer. Here, in a coldly practical way, the necessity of someone like Tyrone Guthrie to the project is evident. Theatre people are the servants of their own reputations; they cannot afford to move far or for long outside the strongest current of their profession. But Guthrie diverts the current to wherever he sets up headquarters; and last summer it was not only artistically rewarding, it was professionally useful, to be working in Minneapolis. I cannot take the space to list the extensive supporting cast; it was clearly of a caliber that could not possibly have been attracted to a typical summer season.

The plays in the maiden year were *Hamlet, The Miser, The Three Sisters,* and *Death of a Salesman.* (The Medici-like largess provided by a well-designed repertory season is shown, I think, by the fact that I arrived in Minneapolis on a Saturday noon, left on Monday morning, and in that span of less than forty-eight hours saw productions of Shakespeare, Molière, and Chekhov. I did not see the Arthur Miller play because it had not yet come into the season.)

And what of the quality of these productions? They have been widely discussed, and I shall not review them systematically here; but, given Guthrie's reputation, they contained surprises. The recurring charge made by his detractors is that Guthrie, for all his loudly avowed

dedication to the classics, shows a lack of respect, verging on contempt, for the texts and intentions of his revered masters. It is implied that his main interest as a director is to prove what a bold, ingenious, and witty showman he can be with familiar material; and the English critic T. C. Worsley has accused him of founding the "Wouldn't It Be Fun (Just For a Change) School of Production." There are horror stories of occasions when whole scenes had to be dropped from a Guthrie production because the willful director had led his cast so far from the true path that the sections in question would be patent absurdities. There is so much smoke of this sort in the theatrical archives that I will not say there is no fire, but I did not find it at Minneapolis.

The two plays staged by Guthrie were *Hamlet* and *The Three Sisters,* and the quality that struck me about both of them was their surpassing legibility. I have seen performances of these works that I thought, in the one case, rose to higher grandeur and, in the other, evoked a more searching poignancy; but I have never seen performances in which the author's design for the structure, the shifting relationships, or the course of the action were more limpidly set forth.

For one thing, *Hamlet* was staged in its entirety, and it became clear that the "versions" of this play when it is trimmed to what is conventionally

deemed a full evening in the theatre are never skillful enough to avoid distortion. To give just one example: when the lines of Claudius are not cropped—as usually they are—it can be seen that, however he acquired the crown, he is a competent king and deeply preoccupied with running his country. Hamlet's obstinate gloom is at first no more than a nuisance to this busy man—it upsets his wife: notice how he keeps the youth waiting until he has disposed of more urgent business. But it is not long before the astute older man senses danger as well as bother in that quarter. Hamlet, after all, is heir to the throne, and murder has a way of begetting murder. If you wonder why Hamlet "hesitates," why he feigns madness, why he runs about so much and buttonholes everyone he meets, consider that he may be trying to kill his uncle without being killed himself. As for Rosencrantz and Guildenstern, who are they but the first and second murderers from *Richard III?* (In Guthrie's sharp business suits, they bear a passing resemblance to Cohn and Schine.)

Those who worry that Guthrie is not respectful enough make a good deal of his enthusiasm for mounting costume plays in modern dress. He defends it on the grounds that the Elizabethans saw their productions so dressed (Shakespeare, after all, was for the most part writing historical plays), and that costumes more familiar than capes and fur-

In an effort to make Shakespeare less starchy and more accessible to today's spectators, Guthrie has sometimes dressed his casts in modern costume and set them against up-to-date scenery. Critics have claimed that this treatment accentuates anachronisms; admirers argue that it gives the plays fresh relevance and power. Guthrie has also altered Gilbert and Sullivan operas, discarding many of their original traditions and making them, perhaps, more understandable to new audiences.

A rollicking H.M.S. Pinafore: *Eric House as Sir Joseph Porter, K.C.B.*

A switch: Voltaire's Candide *with Bernstein's music and Broadway cast*

belows convey quickly to the audience such relevant information as time, place, and the social position of the wearer. Probably so, though modern dress is a manner of speaking; in *Hamlet*, as in other Guthrie productions I have seen, the style is scarcely what you would expect to meet with in Mamaroneck. It is exceedingly elegant, uniforms of Ruritanian bravura abound, formal dress is observed in almost all scenes, and the general atmosphere is certainly elevated, if no longer antiquated. The occasional suitcase, tennis racket, binoculars, or pearl-handled revolver probably calls more attention to itself than its function in the scene is worth.

As for the title role, George Grizzard played with an impressive sense of what it means to be a handsome, rich, and powerful young man with the burden of a considerable tradition resting on his shoulders. His manners were excellent, his wit was quick, he was graceful, tough, daring, and honest—a formidable youth, as his foster father was only too well aware. With Grizzard at the focus, the production became a descriptive *Hamlet* rather than a soaring one, and Guthrie told me later that he worked consciously for an expository quality—an emphasis on what the play is *about*—for playgoers, many of whom would be seeing a Shakespeare text come to life for the first time. Grizzard's voice has not much range and some of the poetry escaped him, but his

speech was decent and it was wonderfully clear. Most important for a young man playing the part for the first time, there was nothing in his interpretation of Hamlet to block its continuing growth—provided, of course, that he ever gets the chance to play it again.

With *The Three Sisters* one comes upon the other side of the open stage versus proscenium argument. Chekhov wrote for the box set; he can be staged on an open platform, but he does not profit thereby. Guthrie admits the problem, but thinks that such plays are not harmed as much as the older classics are helped by his architecture; that to the degree that open staging shifts the feel from realism toward ritual there is a gain. The argument will not become acute until such time as the platform gains the near monopoly that the proscenium has held for two hundred years.

The atmosphere of Chekhov is not dissipated in the arena theatre. The isolation, the taut futility, the closeness of minds and bodies, can be expressed as well on a platform as behind a frame. It is a matter of furniture (in this case ringing the edges and facing into the center), lighting, and the attitudes of the players—hunched shoulders bring the claustrophobia close in. What bothered me was a seeming confusion in the cross-currents of the play. With Shakespeare the structure of intercourse is relatively

formal and simple. You have mob scenes or you have duets, trios, sometimes quartets. An actor is in the action or out of it, and the lines guide the eye. But with Chekhov everyone is constantly involved, currents are moving simultaneously in many directions, and it is not safe to assume that the lines define the action. In that situation a proscenium stage offers the audience a better chance to keep its eye on the whole tableau. The possibilities of grouping and movement are certainly limited, sometimes awkward, and for that reason theatre people get very weary of their box sets. But I found in *The Three Sisters* a tendency for the stage to begin swirling in a slow whirlpool, and I do not think Chekhov wanted any such vertigo. I sometimes lost track of a character important to me, I could not be sure that a quick glance hadn't been masked. Guthrie says that it is a much more relaxed and natural production than could be put onto a conventional stage; very likely, but the price I think is that a new, and unmeant, strain is put on the audience.

It was a lovely, gentle performance, and in this third offering of the first season, Guthrie began to evoke a "company" flavor. It is a quality as elusive as the bouquet of wine; the audience feels it as a sense of well-being: these players know and trust one another, and each dares to give what is within him without reserve. Guthrie defines a great

Guthrie, like his audiences, never seems to tire of Hamlet. *His three most famous mountings of this sturdy war horse have been notable for the clarity with which the text and action were presented, for the furnishings (in what might be called Baroque Modern), and for polished performances in the secondary as well as the main roles. One Ontario player, asked when he had become an actor, replied: "When I started to work for Guthrie."*

Hamlet, *1937, with Laurence Olivier (at far left)*

director as a great audience—an audience of one for whom the players will unfold themselves to the maximum. One felt that *The Three Sisters* was being played for that audience.

Chekhov's humor came through like a chime; the tragedy was perhaps a little conventional, lacking the bittersweet quality of Chekhov's disillusioned compassion. The play can cut deeper into one's heart, but it was nevertheless performed here with exemplary style and feeling. It showed what Chekhov thought of his people, even if it may not have shown everything he felt about them.

The third production of my weekend in Minneapolis was directed by Douglas Campbell; it was the one which, with some justice, might have been criticized on grounds usually used against Guthrie. *The Miser* was handsome to the point of being gorgeous (styled, it is said, after Picasso's *Three Musicians*), pitched in a key of unflagging hilarity, and run off at the speed of a patter song. It was also excessively busy, a little strident, and apparently determined, by inventive stage business and an incipient hysteria, to make up for Molière's inadequacies as a writer of farce .This is not entirely fair to Campbell; he had a difficult problem in that *The Miser* as written does not quite fill an evening, and there were probably not the resources this first season to polish up a curtain raiser. Padding

was needed, and once you start padding Molière with dances, dumb shows, and double-takes, it is hard to draw the line.

Nevertheless the tone seemed to me unnecessarily sweet and creamy. Molière was a satirist, not a confectioner. The cast was campaigning for laughter; whereas a more confident farce group will fend it off, knowing from the bitter experience of clowns that the laughs will not be denied. Thus, Hume Cronyn, who can move with a virtuoso cunning unmatched on the American stage, appeared at times to be racing around the platform in imitation of Bobby Clark chasing his own tail. He was great fun to watch, but the cast seemed to be watching him, too.

It must be said, though, that Campbell knows his audience; *The Miser* was the hit of the season. To be accurate, the Tyrone Guthrie Theatre was the hit of Minnesota and the states bordering thereon. How could these heartland Americans have guessed that anything so sumptuous, so intelligent, so overwhelmingly alive would spring up in their midst? Someone who wasn't born yesterday decided that for the preview performances of *Hamlet* and *The Miser* the invitation audience should be composed of the carpenters, plumbers, electricians, and truck drivers who had worked on the building, plus their wives, and as many local bellhops, desk clerks, and taxi drivers as the premises would hold. I talked

to no plumbers or carpenters but spent a good deal of time in hotels and taxis. The word "Guthrie" seemed to work faster than a tip.

Guthrie had left before I arrived; he was, in fact, off to Ireland to preside at a meeting of a jam factory he had been instrumental in starting in County Monaghan as a device for slowing the sad migration of rural youth to the scant promise of the Irish cities. (The jam, he promises, will be excellent and hideously expensive.) However, I caught up with him in New York. It was early on a very hot morning, and Sir Tyrone received me in a cotton wrapper. In this pseudo-Roman garb, and with his height and near-Cyrano profile, he gave me a vivid, if incongruous, flash of Charles de Gaulle. I wondered how many of his Minneapolis associates, who refer to him so cosily as Tony, call him that to his face. He is an easy man to like, but I should not find it easy to get matey with him.

I asked Guthrie some obvious questions and got better answers than I deserved. How had he decided upon the plays for the first season? The first consideration was not to patronize. You don't ask people to build you a $2,000,000 playhouse in order to give them *Three Men on a Horse* (not, he added hastily, that it isn't a dandy play). At the same time the people of Minneapolis are intelligent but not theatrically knowing—they would probably not accept

amlet, 1938, with Alec Guinness (in white shirt)

Hamlet, 1963, with George Grizzard

avant-garde work. In that situation the safe choice is the very best. Therefore, *Hamlet*. And once you have chosen *Hamlet* you need relief; therefore (also the very best) *The Miser*. Then it becomes a question of seeing what other works of excellence, preferably from different periods, your cast of the first two plays would fit most efficiently. In this case the jigsaw worked best with *The Three Sisters* and *Death of a Salesman*.

I asked him why for the role of Hamlet he had chosen George Grizzard, an actor known previously for his roles in such contemporary plays as *The Desperate Hours, Big Fish, Little Fish,* and *Who's Afraid of Virginia Woolf?* Guthrie replied: he has a quick wit and he wanted to do it. I had not thought of it before, but what sets Hamlet apart from his associates at Elsinore is not that he is gloomier than anyone else but that he can think circles around the lot of them. Grizzard's fast mind is the key to his interpretation.

Then I asked Guthrie what he would like to show Minneapolis next. Something by Ibsen (Minnesota is Scandinavian country); Ben Johnson's *Volpone*; one or another of the restoration comedies (all fine for the open stage, he says, because basically ritual and entirely without illusion); and something from the 1930's in the style of that period— maybe *Dinner at Eight* with elaborate sets rolling in on trucks.

Would he hire the same company next year? Not necessarily. Guthrie's idea of repertory is something between the pure hazard of the commercial theatre and the utter security (boredom) of a resident company. He believes in yearly contracts, to be renewed at the pleasure of actor or management. That way you have a nucleus to start each season, and there are enough new faces to keep things bright. He doubted that the Cronyns would be back next season, though he very much hoped to see them in Minneapolis four or five years from now.

But of course four or five years from now Guthrie himself will not be in Minneapolis. Will the theatre survive without him? I didn't ask him that question; what could he say? No one is indispensable; but Guthrie is a large man, and he designs on a very large scale. His theatres do not grow to maturity; they are born full-grown, and their roots are not deep enough for their spreading aspirations. Guthrie is clearly aware of the danger; he worries about the vitality of the monuments of which he has been the master builder. On the occasion of the Canadian Stratford's tenth anniversary, last summer, he was worrying to this effect in *The New York Times Magazine*, and in that instance he threw the challenge to the audience. Is it self-generating, is it serious (not snobbish but committed), will it open itself to the sort of training in the great past that a repertory

company can offer, and must offer, if it is to extend and deepen its range?

The festival theatre, Guthrie pointed out, is the successor to the road company. The players once came to the people; now the people come to the players. The switch occurred because we have become an incredibly mobile society—it is much easier these days to draw an audience from five states than it is to move a stage production through those five states. And a festival can offer a level of performance and an elegance of occasion quite beyond the expectations of the "national companies" of Broadway hits.

Given the decade at Stratford, and the combination of local civic pride and country-wide applause that made the first Minneapolis season glow, Guthrie is carefully optimistic. "If the theatre is to survive," he says, "it can only be as something more serious and interesting than Showbiz. . . . This presupposes some responsibility—maybe not even that, maybe no more than common sense —on the part of both feeders and fed, in order that the diet be both agreeable and nourishing." Theatre stars are said to be arrogant, but there is modesty as well as generosity in that statement. Guthrie is more than a star; perhaps he is what he set out to be—an artist.

Robert Hatch, a frequent contributor to HORIZON *on the theatre, discussed the art of Orson Welles in the July, 1963, issue.*

Poetry's False Face

By ROBERT GRAVES

Craft, and not mere technique,
is what this English poet-craftsman praises;
for technique is not enough

God, according to a Hebrew myth, promised our father Adam the helpmeet he needed, and invited him to watch while the divine fingers built up a woman's anatomy from primeval sludge. They extemporized bones, tissues, muscles, blood, teeth, brains, and glandular secretions, wove them neatly together, co-ordinated their functions, covered the whole ingenious apparatus with the smoothest of cuticles, and embellished it with tufts of hair in selected places. This technical demonstration caused Adam such disgust that, when the First Eve stood up in all her beauty and smiled at him, he turned his back on her. God therefore removed the First Eve and behaved with greater circumspection: He formed the Second Eve from Adam's rib while he slept, then ordered the Archangel Michael to adorn her in bridal array. Adam woke and was enchanted.

I inherit Adam's mistrust of creative technique. It is grammarians, not poets, who lay down the rules of prosody, name meters, list different varieties of poetic license—deducing them from Greek, Latin, Italian, or French practice—as of universal application. English criticism began in Tudor times with the grammarians; and though some, such as Puttenham, realized that English poetry had its own wayward genius, different from that of the Romance languages, they nevertheless agreed that it must be intellectually disciplined and dedicated to certain social uses. Among these, Puttenham instances the Reporting of the Famous Acts of Princes, the Reproval of Vice, the Treatment of Honest and Profitable Arts and Sciences, Rejoicings at Marriages, Memorials of the Dead. Puttenham links poetic art so securely with the art of rhetoric that when he has discussed the mathematical rules of meter and proportion, which ensure sweet and tuneful sounds, he next turns to the problem of poetic ornament:

And as we see in these great Mesdames of honor, be they for personage or otherwise never so comely and beautiful, yet if they want their courtly habiliments, or at leastwise such other apparel as custom and civility have ordained to cover their naked bodies, would be half-ashamed or greatly out of countenance to be seen in that sort, and perchance do then think themselves more amiable in every man's eye, when they be in their richest attire, suppose of silks or tissues and costly embroideries, than when they go in cloth or in any plain and simple apparel. Even so cannot our . . . Poesie show itself either gallant or gorgeous, if any limb be left naked and bare and not clad in his kindly clothes and colors, such as may convey them somewhat out of sight, that is from the common course of ordinary speech and capacity of the vulgar judgment, and yet being artificially handled must needs yield it much more beauty and commendation. This ornament we speak of is given to it by figures and figurative speeches, which be the flowers as it were and colors that a Poet setteth upon his language by art, as the embroiderer doth his stones and pearls . . . upon the stuff of a Princely garment. . . .

Ornament, as such, should not concern poets, although completely naked poems spring only from extreme passion in love or war. It is true that beautiful women, because of "custom or civility"—not to mention variations of climate—wear clothes as a rule; yet, if truly beautiful and not mere lumps of handsome flesh, they dress for their own pleasure, rather than letting fashion designers (even the Archangel Michael himself) bedizen them for Adam's gratification. And any jewel a woman wears is not mere ornament but a chosen extension of her inner loveliness.

Grammarians insist that a simple idea may be so ornamented by artifice as to become poetic, and that the reader must applaud the ingenuity of its transformation. Poetical artifice entered our universities from Rome by way of

France; Ovid and Virgil were the masters on whom all students must model themselves. Ovid wrote in the *Fasti*:

> *Tres ubi Luciferos veniens praemiserit Eos*
> *tempora nocturnis aequa diurna feres.*
> *Inde quater pastor saturos ubi clauserit haedos,*
> *canuerint herbae rore recente quater,*
> *Ianus adorandus cumque hoc Concordia mitis. . . .*

"When the breaking dawn shall have sent before her three light-bearing days, thou wilt have the hours of day equal to those of night; and when from this the shepherd shall four times have penned his well-fed kids, four times the grass become white with fresh-fallen dew, then Janus and with him mild Concordia will demand adoration. . . ."

In simple English: "Three days later comes the vernal equinox; after four more, the feasts of Janus and Concord will be celebrated." Note the superfluousness of the adjectives—*breaking* dawn, *well-fed* kids, *fresh-fallen* dew, *mild* Concord. Every dawn "breaks"; and even if all the shepherd's kids were not "well fed," their hungry bleatings would not affect the calendar; dew is always "fresh-fallen," and Concord always "mild." In any case Ovid was writing not for shepherds, but for Augustus's city courtiers—few of whom can ever have seen the inside of a goat pen.

Sir Philip Sidney, in his *Apology for Poetry,* accepts this whole cosmetic parlor of classical verse technique as necessary for the production of rich conceits that guide man's soul to moral virtue, courage, and erudition; adding, however:

Certainly I must confess my own barbarousness. I never heard the old song of Percy and Douglas ["Chevy Chase"] that I found not my heart moved more than with a trumpet; and yet is it sung but by some blind crowder with no rougher voice than rude style: which being so evil apparelled in the dust and cobwebs of that uncivil age, what would it work trimmed in the gorgeous eloquence of Pindar?

Now, Pindar could never have begun a poem with:

> *Earl Percie of Northumberland*
> *A vow to God did make . . .*

but would have written:

O Queenly Muse, our Mother, come, I beseech thee, on the festal day of the Omnipotent Christ-child who bountifully redeemed us from sin: come visiting the spacious halls of our impregnable New Castle that beetles in majesty above the goodly Tynian water. For lo, youthful craftsmen of honey-sweet triumphal songs, skilled also in laments, there attend in long desire for thy voice. Various deeds thirst for various rewards, yet the hunting of high-stepping, lotus-cropping deer that rove the rugged Cheviotian hills, calleth beyond all things for the meed of song, especially when mighty champions contend together in honor, each assuring for himself the certain glory of carrying home in well-wrought horse-drawn wains tasty haunches of unnumbered antlered ones.

It would have taken Pindar a whole page to trim with gorgeous eloquence such stanzas as these:

> *It began upon a Monnynday,*
> *Ere daylight did appear;*
> *The drivers through the woodës went*
> *To raise the fallow deer.*

> *The bowmen cleft them to the hearts*
> *As down the brae they came;*
> *And greyhounds through the greves did rin:*
> *To them it was good game.*

Two centuries later, Dr. Johnson wrote about "Chevy Chase":

[Addison] descended now and then to lower disquisitions [than his praise of Milton]; and by a serious display of the beauties of "Chevy Chase" he exposed himself to the ridicule of Wagstaff . . . and to the contempt of Dennis, who, considering the fundamental position of his criticism that "Chevy Chase" pleases, and ought to please, because it is natural, observes, "that there is a way of deviating from nature, by bombast or tumor, which soars above nature, and enlarges images beyond their real bulk; by affectation, which forsakes nature in quest of something unsuitable; and by imbecility, which degrades nature by faintliness and diminution, by obscuring its appearances, and weakening its effects." In "Chevy Chase" there is not much of either bombast or affectation; but there is a chill, lifeless imbecility. The story cannot possibly be told in a manner that shall make less impression on the mind.

The classicists thus ask us to choose between the "chill and lifeless imbecility" of "Chevy Chase" and such supreme excellence as Addison's "Letter from Italy" which, Dr. Johnson says, has "always been praised, but has never been praised beyond its merit. It is more correct, with less appearance of labor, and more elegant, with less ambition of ornament, than any of his other poems."

Pindar may have been praised by Sir Philip Sidney for his "gorgeous eloquence," but he could take a whole page just to get a poem started.

Though among "the masters" on whom students are supposed to model themselves, Ovid piled up exquisite adjectives in rural poems for city-bred Roman courtiers.

A LETTER FROM ITALY

(To the Right Hon. Charles Lord Halifax, 1701)

While you my lord the rural shades admire,
And from Britannia's public posts retire;
No longer, her ungrateful sons to please,
For their advantage sacrifice your ease;
Me into foreign realms my fate conveys,
Through nations fruitful of immortal lays,
Where the soft season and inviting clime
Conspire to trouble your repose with rhyme. . . .

I have elsewhere explained the difference between Apollonian poetry and Muse poetry.* That Pindar and Addison claim to have the Muse in their pockets complicates the situation. Yet the truth is that "Chevy Chase" moved Sir Philip Sidney's heart more than a trumpet because the unknown rude crowder who composed it was himself so moved, and that the Apollonians decry all emotional impulses which have not been modified and ennobled, after a grounding in the humanities, by the acquisition of classical technique. Technique should not be equated with craftsmanship. Technique is psychological know-how. The technician assumes that poems can be constructed like explosive missiles and aimed at a given target; he despises mere craftsmen for their intellectual sloth. Eliot, Pound, and the later Yeats (still praised by English and American literary journals as the "real masters") have technique; Hardy and Frost had only craftsmanship. (As the Three Wise Men might have said apologetically to Joseph and Mary: "We bring only gold, myrrh, and frankincense.")

Technique ignores the factor of magic; craftsmanship pre-

* See *The White Goddess* (Farrar, Straus & Cudahy, 1948).

supposes it. A journeyman, after seven years as apprentice, will get the feel of his materials and learn what quiet miracles can be done with them. A small part of this knowledge is verbally communicable; the rest is incommunicable—except to fellow craftsmen who already possess it. The technician's disregard of this inexplicable element, magic, in painting, sculpture, medicine, music, and poetry—on the grounds that it cannot be demonstrated under laboratory conditions—accounts for the present dismal decline in all arts. A true poem is best regarded as already existing before it has been composed, with composition as the act of deducing its entirety from a single key phrase that swims into the poet's mind.

Here are two well-known pieces of Tennyson's, "The Eagle" and " 'Move, Eastward, Happy Earth,' " printed on the same page in his Collected Poems and forced on me, when I was seven or eight years old, as works of genius. "The Eagle" is subtitled 'Fragment,' suggesting that a longer poem went wrong and that he destroyed all but six sound lines. Whenever this happens to a poet, he should justify by careful craftsmanship the publication of what is salvaged. But has Tennyson done so?

He clasps the crag with crooked hands;
Close to the sun in lonely lands,
Ring'd with the azure world, he stands.
The wrinkled sea beneath him crawls;
He watches from his mountain walls,
And like a thunderbolt he falls.

My minimum requirement of a poem is that it should make prose sense as well as poetic sense, one main difference between prose and poetry being that prose engages only a small part of the reader's attention. Ideally, a poem should induce in him the same trance of heightened sensibility under which the poet wrote, and make him aware of all the multiple meanings that stretch out in vistas from it. Here, Tennyson's technique has been deliberately impressionistic—he has, in fact, taken no pains to say what he means—and, although his resonant voice with the slight Norfolk burr might have persuaded his hearers that these two stanzas make prose sense (the ear being easily deceived), the reading eye rejects them.

Persistent alliteration pleases children, who enjoy "one old ox opening oysters" and "two toads terribly tired, trying to trot to Tilbury." And it pleased simple Anglo-Saxons:

With Vandals I was and with Vaerns and Vikings;
With Saxons I was, and with Syegs and Swordsmen;
With Franks I was, with Frisians and Frumtings. . . .

But when, in a Victorian three-line rhyming stanza, four *c*'s appear in a row—*clasp, crag, crooked,* and *close*—followed by the two *l*'s of *lonely lands,* we expect the last line to yield an important and equally alliterative statement:

He clasps the crag with crooked hands;
Close to the sun in lonely lands . . .

Yet,

> *Ring'd with the azure world, he stands . . .*

disappoints expectation, and adds nothing to the picture. Since the eagle perches on his crag close to the sun, a background of blue sky has already been presumed. Besides, it is not the *world* which is blue, but only the sky. And why "he clasps the crag with crooked *hands?*" Though few men are born with prehensile feet, "hands" might still have passed muster in a portrait of this humanized eagle, had Tennyson not followed it with "he stands." If the eagle stands on his hands, then his wings must necessarily be feet. . . .

Once one thinks along these lines, the poem collapses. *Crooked* is unnecessary: eagles' claws are always crooked. *Lands* is seen to be a rhyme chosen to go with *hands* and *stands*; for the eagle can stand only in one land, not several. To present him as "close to the sun" is hardly fair—what are a few hundred feet, compared with 92,000,000 miles! Nor is he even flying high above the mountain, but grounded on a crag. . . .

Azure is a purely heraldic term for "blue," and if Tennyson thought of the eagle as a heraldic charge—*Azure: below a sun in its splendor Or, an eagle of the same, ungled and langed Argent*—he should have made this clear. *Ringed with azure* is not the language of heraldry.

> *The wrinkled sea beneath him crawls;*
> *He watches from his mountain walls,*
> *And like a thunderbolt he falls.*

Why is the bird's attention concentrated on the sea? Is he perhaps a sea eagle, watching for fish? *Crawls* may mean that from a great height waves appear to move slowly; but since *wrinkles* are by definition static, *crawls* must have been put there for the rhyme. And unless we are told exactly what the eagle is watching, his fall could have been as accidental as was, say, Eutychus's when Paul's sermon sent him to sleep and he crashed onto the street from an upper window. Tennyson has a vague sense, perhaps, of the eagle as a royal bird mythologically entitled—like Solar Jove, his master—to a blue nimbus and a thunderbolt. If so, he does not make the point. He would have done better with:

JOVE'S EAGLE

> *Charged on an azure field, with claws*
> *Grasping a crag, he overawes*
> *(Like Jove himself) the doves and daws.*
>
> *Silently watches from his walls*
> *What swims the sea, what flies, what crawls—*
> *Ere like a thunderbolt he falls.*

This is still not a poem. I have indulged Tennyson by granting him his Victorian *daws* and his *Ere*; nor do I much like the similarity of these two sets of rhymes; but at least the verses now make immediate prose sense and would serve well enough as an anthology piece.

Now for its companion verse:

> *Move eastward, happy earth, and leave*
> *Yon orange sunset waning slow:*
> *From fringes of the faded eve,*
> *O happy planet, eastward go,*
>
> *Till over thy dark shoulder glow*
> *Thy silver sister-world, and rise*
> *To glass herself in dewy eyes*
> *That watch me from the glen below.*
>
> *Ah, bear me with thee, smoothly borne,*
> *Dip forward under starry light,*
> *And move me to my marriage-morn,*
> *And round again to happy night.*

The gist is: "I shall be so happy when the sunset has ended; when tonight's moon has come and gone, and morning is here, and I am married to Maud, and—oh, tomorrow night!"

Nobody can put this poem right. It would have to be rewritten as a popular song:

> *O tomorrow night,*
> *O tomorrow night,*
> *I'll be so happy when today is done,*
> *And I've said goodbye to the dear old sun . . .*

That an eager lover should apostrophize the weather to be fine on his wedding day, and the birds to wake him early, and the countryside to rejoice, is understandable. Lovers always take the weather personally. But when Earth is begged to dip forward and carry the poet along with smooth and careful portage for another twenty-four hours or so! "Move eastward, happy earth . . ." and "O happy planet, eastward go," though parallel orders, are far from explicit.

Of Addison's "Letter from Italy," Dr. Johnson said it has "always been praised, but has never been praised beyond its merit." Mr. Graves thinks otherwise.

"Eastward of what must I dip, Mr. Tennyson?" Mother Earth has a right to ask.

Shelley is another culprit:

TO A SKYLARK

Hail to thee, blithe Spirit!
Bird thou never wert,
That from Heaven, or near it,
Pourest thy full heart
In profuse strains of unpremeditated art.

Higher still and higher
From the earth thou springest
Like a cloud of fire;
The deep blue thou wingest,
And singing still dost soar, and soaring ever singest.

In the golden lightning
Of the sunken sun,
O'er which clouds are bright'ning,
Thou dost float and run;
Like an unbodied joy whose race is just begun.

The pale purple even
Melts around thy flight;
Like a star of Heaven,
In the broad daylight
Thou art unseen—but yet I hear thy shrill delight,

* * *

Like a Poet hidden
In the light of thought,
Singing hymns unbidden,
Till the world is wrought
To sympathy with hopes and fears it heeded not:

Tennyson, in one poem, has "taken no pains to say what he means." Perhaps his "resonant voice" could have made his verse make sense to the ear, if not to the mind.

* * *

Chorus Hymeneal,
Or triumphal chant,
Matched with thine would be all
But an empty vaunt,
A thing wherein we feel there is some hidden want.

What objects are the fountains
Of thy happy strain?
What fields, or waves, or mountains?
What shapes of sky or plain?
What love of thine own kind? what ignorance of pain?

It is a temptation to let Shelley off; but the "Skylark" ranks among the shoddiest poems ever wished on us as the product of genius. Its meter is difficult, granted. Yet with faith in the power of inspiration to solve all problems of craftsmanship, a poet may commit himself to a metrical scheme that seems cripplingly tight and yet feel free as air within it. Shelley, it seems, snatched idly at an idea that entered his head one afternoon as he tried to locate a lark singing in the sky, and began with:

Hail to thee, blithe Spirit!
All unseen thou art,
That from Heaven, or near it,
Pourest thy full heart
In happy strains of unpremeditated art.

In the golden lightning
Of the setting sun,
Which the clouds is brightening,
Thou dost float and run. . . .

Shelley goes home, fetches pencil and notebook, and jots down this much; but then discovers that he has rhymed *thou art* with *unpremeditated art*—which is a "French rhyme" disallowed to English poets since Chaucer's time. One of the two *arts* must be struck out. So, having decided that the meter cannot be managed without recourse to near rhymes like *wrought* and *not; spirit* and *near it; chant, vaunt,* and *want;* he pencils the rhyme scheme in the margin, and changes his original *All unseen thou art* to *Bird thou never wert,* a dramatic statement irreconcilable with his later suggestion that the cock-lark's song is prompted by love for his hen. Nevertheless, he reserves *Unseen thou art* and *happy strain* for a subsequent verse.

A second difficulty is the golden light*ning* of the sett*ing* sun brighten*ing* the clouds. Too many *ings*! He toys with his pencil, scratches his head, peels a grape, eats it, looks out of the window at the sun, and sees that it has sunk almost below the horizon. So *sunken sun,* instead of *setting sun,* gets rid of one *ing;* but he had forgotten that, unlike nightingales, larks never sing in a darkened sky, and that clouds never brighten once the sun has disappeared, but turn a dingy red. No matter! The stars are coming out one by one, and it occurs to him that though an hour or two ago the lark was invisible even by broad daylight, neither could he see a single star. So, vaguely remembering the Bible verse about the morning stars that sing together, and the sons of God who shout for joy, he conflates the lark with the star into a single blithe Spirit springing like a fiery cloud higher and higher, while the pale purple evening melts around it, like a poet hidden in the light of thought. This confused image has been much admired; but true poetic ecstasy makes sense, and more than sense.

The rhymes *higher–fire, springest–wingest–singest, heaven–even, hidden–unbidden,* are borrowings from the hymnal, and not long before his death Shelley thought seriously of becoming an Anglican clergyman. Here he pictures the poet as an amateur hymnologist: singing hymns unbidden. There is something, I own, that endears Shelley to us—a generous-hearted muddle; and the patent clumsiness of "To a Skylark" makes us feel for him as for a child of ten who has painted a sunset picture, thinks it wonderful, and wants to be praised. We paste it into the family scrapbook and he signs his name to it in large, round characters. "Nice fellow," we say, years later, "good Classic, went to Eton and Oxford, turned out neat translations from the Greek dramatists. Wouldn't hurt a fly; a bit of a radical, of course. Sent down from Univ. for atheism. Pity! Deucedly odd at times—believe it or not, he used to put revolutionary broadsheets into empty wine bottles and throw them into the Bristol Channel, hoping that they might float across to Ireland! Wrote a sonnet about 'em too, beginning:

> *Vessels of heavenly medicine! may the breeze*
> *Auspicious waft your dark green forms to shore;*
> *Safe may ye stem the wide surrounding roar*
> *Of the wild whirlwinds and the raging seas;*
> *And oh! if Liberty e'er deigned to stoop*
> *From yonder lowly throne her crownless brow,*
> *Sure she will breathe around your emerald group*
> *The fairest breezes of her west that blow. . . .*

Sure, he got the color right: Erin's own emerald. But why did he call for westerly breezes instead of easterly ones? Poetic license, perhaps. Got drowned sailing in the Mediterranean. Sad, but hardly surprising!"

By way of contrast, a glorious example of how inspiration can make light of severe metrical discipline is Bernard de Cluny's twelfth-century *De Contemptu Mundi,* from which J. M. Neale adapted the hymn "Jerusalem the Golden, with Milk and Honey Blest":

> *Urbs Sion aurea, patria lactea, cive decora,*
> *Omne cor obruis, omnibus obstruis et cor et ora.*
> *Nescio, nescio quae jubilatio, lux tibi qualis,*
> *Quam socialia gaudia, gloria quam specialis.*

> * * *

> *Sunt Sion atria conjubilantia, martyre plena,*
> *Cive micantia, principe stantia, luce serena. . . .*

We may find Shelley endearing, "a generous-hearted muddle," but "To a Skylark," in Graves's opinion, "ranks among the shoddiest poems ever wished on us as the product of genius."

Technically, the meter is called *Lenonini cristati trilices dactylia;* and Bernard has told how, though the Holy Spirit often begged him to write verses, he would not listen until the sudden cry came: "Open the door to thy Beloved!" Then Bernard gave way, praying for heavenly grace that he might worthily sing his Beloved's praises. "Open thy mouth," he heard again, and felt inspiration breathed into him. Bernard writes:

And I say in no wise arrogantly, but with all humility and therefore boldness: that unless the Spirit of wisdom and understanding had been with me, and flowed in upon so difficult a meter, I could never have composed so long a work. . . .

For *De Contemptu Mundi* runs for some three thousand lines without flagging. We need not question Bernard's testimony that he wrote in an ecstatic love trance. There can be no other explanation. If only Shelley had written "To a Skylark" under the same spell.

The classical convention in English poetry broke down just before the First World War, and all subsequent attempts to reinstate it failed. Our modernists are still in desperate search for a new convention of equal nonsensicality, yet of international prestige, which will create the impression that they are poets "hidden in the light of thought." But what *objects* are the fountains of their doleful strain? Apparently the sole object is *technique,* which they have made almost a dirty word.

Robert Graves, one of Britain's foremost poets and men of letters, concludes with this article his recent series of Oxford lectures on English poetry. Two previous essays appeared in the HORIZON *issues for March and May, 1963.*

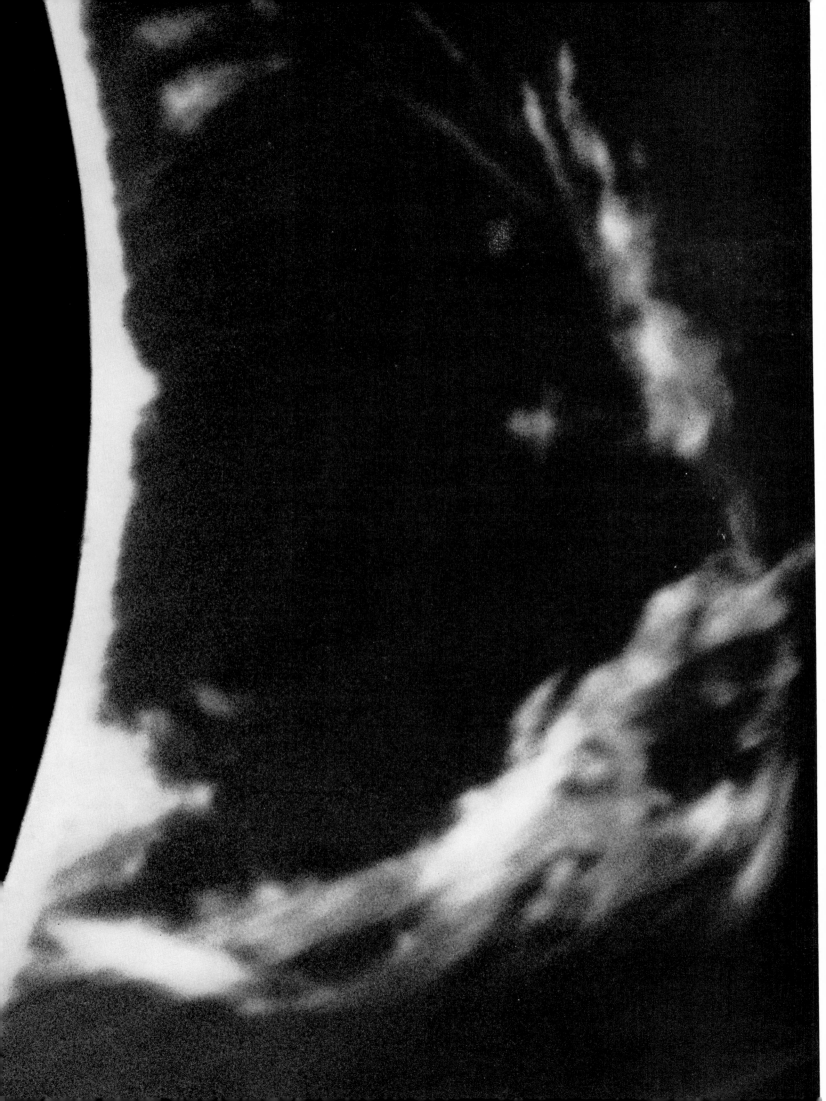

Is it old? Absolutely. At least 5,000,000,000 years.
Relatively? As one week in the life of man. We are creatures
of the dawn. It will grow colder, but we may move closer

By ARTHUR C. CLARKE

IN THE LIGHT OF THE SUN

Ra, the Egyptian sun-god

The only sun that can be "seen" is the scientific one, photographed in but a narrow fraction of its light and often (opposite) with its disc eclipsed, so that the hundreds-of-thousands-of-miles-high "prominences" are all that appear. For the most part, men have had to see the sun in symbols; a selection of them—from ancient to modern—follows on subsequent pages.

No man has ever seen the Sun, or ever will. What we call "sunlight" is only a narrow span of the entire solar spectrum—the immensely broad band of vibrations which the Sun, our nearest star, pours into space. All the colors visible to the eye, from warm red to deepest violet, lie within a single octave of this band—for the waves of violet light have twice the frequency, or "pitch" if we think in musical terms, of red. On either side of this narrow zone are ranged octave after octave of radiations to which we are totally blind.

The musical analogy is a useful one. Think of one octave on the piano—less than the span of the average hand. Imagine that you were deaf to all notes outside this range; how much, then, could you appreciate of a full orchestral score when everything from contra bassoon to piccolo is going full blast? Obviously you could get only the faintest idea of the composer's intentions. In the same way, by eye alone we can obtain only a grossly restricted conception of the true "color" of the world around us.

However, let us not exaggerate our visual handicap. Though visible light is merely a single octave of the sun's radiation, it does contain most of the power; the higher and lower frequencies are relatively feeble. It is, of course, no coincidence that our eyes are adapted to the most intense band of sunlight; if that band had been somewhere else in the spectrum—as is the case with other stars—evolution would have given us eyes appropriately tuned.

Nevertheless, the sun's invisible rays are extremely important, and affect our lives in ways undreamed of until only a few years ago. Some of them, indeed, may control our destinies—and even, as we shall see in a moment, our very existence.

The visible spectrum is, quite arbitrarily, divided up into seven primary colors—the famous sequence red, orange, yellow, green, blue, indigo, violet, if we start from the longest waves and work down to the shortest. Seven main colors in the one octave; but the complete band of solar radia-

Thanks to special photographic films, we have all had glimpses of the world of infrared. It is an easily recognizable world, though tone values are strangely distorted. Sky and water are black, leaves and grass dazzlingly white, as if covered with snow. It is a world of clear, far horizons, for infrared rays slice through the normal haze of distance—hence their great value in aerial photography.

The farther we go down into the infrared, the stranger are the sights we encounter and the harder it becomes to relate them to the world of our normal senses. It is only very recently (partly under the spur of guided-missile development) that we have

strike at them even in complete darkness. Only in the last decade have our guided missiles learned the same trick.

Below the infrared, for several octaves, is a no man's land of radiation about which very little is known. It is hard to generate or to detect waves in this region, and until recently few scientists paid it much attention. But as we press on to longer and longer waves we come at last to more familiar territory; first we encounter the inch-long wave of radar, then the yard-long one of the short-wave bands, then the hundred-yard wave of the broadcast band.

The existence of all these radiations was quite unknown a century ago; today, of

Sumerian sun, c. 2700 B.C.

Old Hopi Indian sun-god

Sun wheel, Konarak, India

tions covers at least thirty octaves, or a total frequency range of ten thousand million to one. If we could see the whole of it, therefore, we might expect to discern more than two hundred colors as distinct from each other as orange is from yellow, or green is from blue.

Starting with the sun's visible rays, let us explore outward in each direction and see (though that word is hardly applicable) what we can discover. On the long-wave side we come first to the infrared rays, which can be perceived by our skin but not by our eyes. For infrared rays are heat radiation; go out of doors on a summer day, and you can tell where the sun is even though your eyes may be tightly clenched.

invented sensing devices that can operate in the far infrared. They see the world of heat; they can "look" at a man wearing a brilliantly colored shirt and smoking a cigarette—and see only the glowing tip. They can also look down on a landscape hidden in the darkness of night, and see all the sources of heat from factories, automobiles, taxiing aircraft. Hours after a jet has taken off, they can still read its signature on the warm runway.

Some animals have developed an infrared sense, to enable them to hunt at night. There is a snake which has two small pits near its nostrils, each holding a directional infrared detector. These allow it to "home" upon small, warm animals like mice, and to

course, they are among the most important tools of our civilization. It is a bare twenty years since we discovered that the Sun also produces them, on a scale we cannot hope to match with our puny transmitters.

The Sun's radio output differs profoundly from its visible light, and the difference is not merely one of greater length. Visible sunlight is practically constant in intensity; if there are any fluctuations, they are too slight to be detected. Not only has the Sun shone with unvarying brightness throughout the whole span of human history, but we would probably notice no difference if we could see it through the eyes of one of the great reptiles.

But if you saw only the "radio" Sun,

you would never guess that it was the same object. Most of the time it is very dim—much dimmer, in fact, than many other celestial bodies. To the eye able to see only by radio waves, there would be little difference between day and night; the rising of the Sun would be a minor and inconspicuous event.

From time to time, however, the radio Sun explodes into nova brightness. It may, within seconds, flare up to a hundred, a thousand, or even a million times its normal brilliance. These colossal outbursts of radio energy do not come from the Sun as a whole, but from small fixed areas of the solar disc, often associated with sunspots.

and radio telescopes dramatize the problem involved. If creatures with radio senses do exist anywhere in the universe, they must be far larger than whales, and can therefore only be inhabitants of gravity-free space.

Meanwhile, back on Earth, let us consider the other end of the spectrum—the rays shorter than visible light. As the blue deepens into indigo and then violet, the human eye soon fails to respond. But there is still "light" present in solar radiation—the ultraviolet. As in the case of the infrared, our skins can react to it, often painfully; for ultraviolet rays are the cause of sunburn.

ferent types of glass and assembled with great care into a single unit. The eye has only one lens, and it already has trouble coping with the two-to-one range of wave lengths in the visible spectrum. You can prove this by looking at a bright red object on a bright blue background. They won't both be in perfect focus; when you look at one, the other will appear to be slightly fuzzy.

Objects would be even fuzzier if we could see by ultraviolet as well as by visible light, so the eye deals with this insolvable problem by eliminating it. There is a filter in the front of the eye which blocks the ultraviolet, preventing it from reaching the

Roman mosaic floor from Egypt

Early American sunflower quilt

Buddhist sun medallion, India

This may be the reason why no animals seem ever to have developed radio senses. Most of the time such a sense would be useless, because the radio landscape would be completely dark—there would be no source of illumination.

In any event, "radio eyes" would pose some major biological problems. Because radio waves are millions of times longer than light waves, the corresponding sense organs would have to be millions of times larger than normal eyes, if they were to have the same definition. Even a radio eye which showed the world as fuzzily as a badly out-of-focus television picture would have to be hundreds of yards in diameter; the gigantic antennas of our radar systems

And here is a very strange and little-known fact. Though I have just stated that our eyes do not respond to ultraviolet, the actual situation is a good deal more complicated. (In nature, it usually is.) The sensitive screen at the back of the eye—the retina, which is the precise equivalent of the film in a camera—*does* react strongly to ultraviolet. If it were the only factor involved, we could see by the invisible ultraviolet rays.

Then why don't we? For a purely technical reason. Though the eye is an evolutionary marvel, it is a very poor piece of optics. To enable it to work properly over the whole range of colors, a good camera has to have four or more lenses, made of dif-

retina. The haze filter that photographers often employ when using color film does exactly the same job, and for a somewhat similar reason.

The eye's filter is the lens itself—and here at last is the punch line of this rather long-winded narrative. If you are ever unlucky enough to lose your natural lenses (say through a cataract operation), and have them replaced by artificial lenses of clear glass, you will be able to see quite well in the ultraviolet. Indeed, with a source of ultraviolet illumination, like the so-called "black light" lamps, you will be able to see perfectly in what is, to the normal person, complete darkness! I hereby donate this valuable information to the C.I.A., Ellery

L. TO R.: LUC JOUBERT—LOUVRE; N.Y. PUB. LIB. PICTURE COLL.; ROGER-VIOLLET;
The Sun in Art, GRAPHIS, ZURICH; N.Y. HISTORICAL ASSOCIATION; *The Art of India:
Temples and Sculpture* BY L. FREDERIC

Queen, or anyone else who is interested.

Normal sunlight, as you can discover during a day at the beach, contains plenty of ultraviolet. It all lies, however, in a narrow band—the single octave just above the visible spectrum in frequency. As we move beyond this to still higher frequencies, the scene suddenly dims and darkens. A being able to see only in the far ultraviolet would be in a very unfortunate position. To him it would always be night, whether or not the sun was above the horizon.

What has happened? Doesn't the Sun radiate in the far ultraviolet? Certainly it does—but this radiation is all blocked by

climbed through the opaque fog of the atmosphere. Beyond this, between twenty and thirty miles high, the ultraviolet sun would break through in its awful glory.

I use that word "awful" with deliberate intent. These rays can kill, and swiftly. They do not bother astronauts because they can be easily filtered out by special glass. But if they were to reach the surface of the earth—if they were not blocked by the upper atmosphere—most existing forms of life would be wiped out.

If you regard the existence of this invisible ultraviolet umbrella as in any way providential, you are confusing cause and effect. The screen was not put in the atmos-

short ultraviolet rays were blocked twenty miles up, did the present types of terrestrial life evolve. If there had been no ozone layer, they would doubtless have evolved into different forms. Perhaps we might still be here, but our skins would be very, very black.

Life on Mars must face this problem, for that planet seems to have no oxygen in its atmosphere, and therefore no ozone layer. The far ultraviolet rays must reach the Martian surface unhindered, and must profoundly affect all living matter there. It has been suggested that these rays are responsible for the color changes which astronomers have observed on the planet.

Aztec sun calendar, A.D.

Greek sun-god from Italy

Albrecht Dürer: woodcut, 1498

the atmosphere, miles above our head. In the far ultraviolet a few inches of ordinary air are as opaque as a sheet of metal.

Only with the development of rocket-borne instruments has it become possible to study this unknown region of the solar spectrum—a region, incidentally, which contains vital information about the Sun and the processes that power its nuclear furnace. If your vision were restricted to the far ultraviolet, and you started off from ground level on a bright, sunny day, this is what you would see.

At first, you would be in utter darkness—even though you were looking straight at the Sun. Then, about twenty miles up, you would notice a slow brightening, as you

phere to protect terrestrial life—it was put there by life itself, hundreds of millions of years before man appeared on Earth.

The Sun's raw ultraviolet rays, in all probability, *did* reach the surface of the primeval Earth; the earliest forms of life were adapted to it—perhaps even thrived upon it. In those days there was no oxygen in the atmosphere; oxygen is a by-product of plant life, and over geological aeons its amount slowly increased—until at last those oxygen-burning creatures called animals had a chance to thrive.

That filter in the sky is made of oxygen—or, rather, the grouping of three oxygen atoms known as ozone. Not until Earth's protective ozone layer was formed, and the

Whether or not this is true, we can predict that one of the occupational hazards of Martian explorers will be severe sunburn.

Just as ultraviolet lies beyond the violet, so beyond the ultraviolet lie still shorter rays. These are X rays, which are roughly a thousand times shorter than visible light. Like the ultraviolet, these even more dangerous rays are blocked by the atmosphere; few of them come to within a hundred miles of Earth, and they have been detected by rocket instruments only during the past few years. The solar X rays are quite feeble—only a millionth of the intensity of visible light—but their importance is much greater than this figure would indicate. We know now that blasts of X rays from the

Sun, impinging upon the upper atmosphere, can produce violent changes in radio communications, even to the extent of complete blackouts. Men have lost their lives because the Sun has disrupted radio; nations are equally vulnerable in this age of the ICBM.

You will recall that though the Sun shines with remarkable steadiness in the visible spectrum, it flares and sparkles furiously on the long (radio) waves. Exactly the same thing happens with its X-ray emission, even though these waves are a billion times shorter. Moreover, both the Sun's radio waves and its X rays appear to come from the same localized

exactly the time when the first major space expeditions are being planned—say around 1968. The astronauts may run into some heavy weather, for by then the Sun will be shooting out not only vast quantities of ultraviolet, X rays, and radio waves, but other radiations which cannot be so easily blocked.

We see, then, how complicated and how variable sunlight is—if we use that word in the widest sense to describe *all* the waves emitted by the Sun. Nevertheless, when we accept the evidence of our unaided eyes and describe the Sun as a yellow star, we have summed up the most important single fact about it—*at this moment in time.*

light is concentrated in the yellow band of the spectrum, falling slowly in intensity toward both the longer and shorter waves.

That yellow "hump" will shift as the Sun evolves, and the light of day will change accordingly. It is natural to assume that as the Sun grows older, and uses up its hydrogen fuel—which it is now doing at the spanking rate of half a billion tons a second—it will become steadily colder and redder.

But the evolution of a star is a highly complex matter, involving chains of interlocking nuclear reactions. According to one theory, the Sun is still growing hotter, and will continue to do so for several bil-

E. Cocker: calligraphic sun, 1657

Alexander Girard: sun, 1960

Saul Steinberg: cartoon detail

areas of the solar surface—disturbed regions in the neighborhood of sunspots, where clouds of incandescent gas larger than the Earth erupt into space at hundreds of miles a second.

For reasons not yet understood (there is not much about the Sun that we do *thoroughly* understand) solar activity rises and falls in an eleven-year cycle. The Sun was most active around 1957—which is why that date was chosen for the International Geophysical Year. Now it is heading for a minimum, and to take advantage of this, scientists are making arrangements for a little IGY called the "Year of the Quiet Sun." It is rather unfortunate that the Sun will be coming back to the boil at

It appears probable, however, that sunlight will be the color we know for only a negligibly small part of the Sun's history.

For stars, like individuals, age and change. As we look out into space, we see around us stars at all stages of evolution. There are faint blood-red dwarfs so cool that their surface temperature is a mere 4,000 degrees Fahrenheit; there are searing ghosts blazing at 100,000 degrees and almost too hot to be seen, for the greater part of their radiation is in the invisible ultraviolet. Obviously, the "daylight" produced by any star depends upon its temperature; today (and for ages past, as for ages to come) our Sun is at about 10,000 degrees Fahrenheit, and this means that most of its

lion years. Probably life will be able to adapt itself to these changes—unless they occur catastrophically, as would be the case if the Sun exploded into a nova. In any event, whatever the vicissitudes of the next five or ten billion years, the Sun will finally settle down to the white-dwarf stage.

It will be a tiny thing, not much bigger than the Earth, and therefore too small to show a disc to the naked eye. At first it will be hotter than it is today, but because of its minute size it will radiate very little heat to its surviving planets. The daylight of that distant age will be as cold as moonlight, but much bluer, and the temperature of the Earth will have fallen to 300 degrees below zero. If you think of mercury lamps

L. TO R.: MUSEO NACIONAL DE ANTHROPOLOGIA, MEXICO CITY; LOUVRE—GIRAUDON;
N.Y. PUB. LIB. PRINT ROOM; VICTORIA AND ALBERT MUSEUM; LA FONDA DEL SOL,
RESTAURANT ASSOCIATES; SAUL STEINBERG

on a freezing winter night, you have a faint mental picture of high noon in the year 7,000,000,000.

Yet that does not mean life—even life as we know it today—will be impossible in the solar system; it will simply have to move in toward the shrunken sun. The construction of artificial planets would be child's play to the intelligences we can expect by that date; indeed, it will be child's play to *us* in a few hundred years time.

Around the year 10,000,000,000 the dwarf Sun will have cooled back to its present temperature, and hence to the yellow color that we know today. From a body that was sufficiently close to it—say only

preciated, results of modern astrophysical theories.

When the Sun shrinks to a dull red dwarf, it will not be dying. It will just be starting to live—*and everything that has gone before will be merely a fleeting prelude to its real history.*

For a red dwarf, because it is so small and so cool, loses energy at such an incredibly slow rate that it can stay in business for thousands of times longer than a normal-sized white or yellow star. We must no longer talk in billions but in trillions of years if we are to measure its life span. Such figures are, of course, inconceivable (for that matter, who can think of a thou-

—but our reaction to it is wholly irrelevant and misleading. For we are creatures of the dawn, with eyes and senses adapted to the hot light of today's primeval Sun. Though we should miss beyond measure the blues and greens and violets that are the fading afterglow of Creation, they are all doomed to pass with the brief billion-year infancy of the stars.

But the eyes that will look upon that all-but-eternal crimson twilight will respond to the colors we cannot see; aeons earlier, evolution will have moved their sensitivity away from the yellow, somewhere out beyond the visible red. The world of rainbow-hued heat they see will

Antonio Frasconi: woodcut, *1953*

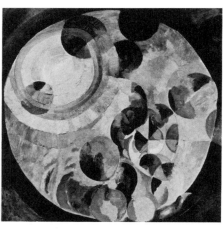

R. Delaunay: Sun and Moon, *1913*

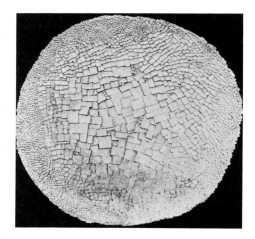

A. L. Toledo Piza: Mosaic #34, *1961*

a million miles away—it would look exactly like our present Sun, and would give just as much heat. There would be no way of telling, by eye alone, that it was actually a hundred times smaller—and a hundred times closer.

So matters may continue for another five billion years; but at last the inevitable will happen. Very slowly, the Sun will begin to cool, dropping from yellow down to red. Perhaps by the year 15,000,000,000 it will become a red dwarf, with a surface temperature of a mere 4,000 degrees. It will be nearing the end of the evolutionary track —but reports of its death will be greatly exaggerated. For now comes one of the most remarkable, and certainly least ap-

sand years?) but we can nevertheless put them into their right perspective if we relate the life of a star to the life of a man.

On this scale, the Sun is but a week old. Its flaming youth will continue for another month; then it will settle down to a sedate, adult existence which may last at least eighty years. Life has existed on this planet for two or three days of the week that has passed; the whole of human history lies within the last second—and there are eighty years to come.

In the wonderful closing pages of *The Time Machine* the young H. G. Wells described the world of the far future, with a blood-red sun hanging over a freezing sea. It is a somber picture that chills the blood

be as rich and colorful as ours—and as beautiful; for a melody is not lost when it is merely transposed an octave down into the bass.

So now we know that Shelley, who was right in so many things, was wrong when he wrote:

Life, like a dome of many-colored glass,
Stains the white radiance of Eternity.

For the radiance of eternity is not white: it is infrared.

For first proposing communication satellites (which he wrote about in HORIZON, *January, 1962), Mr. Clarke was awarded a Gold Medal by the Franklin Institute, Philadelphia.*

POKER
and American Character

Once the proud diversion of self-reliant,
democratic man, the great game is dying out in the land
of its birth, done in by women, wild cards,
military strategists, and the hunger for security

By JOHN LUKACS

The origins of poker are very obscure: encyclopedias and dictionaries give either vague or contradictory information about its origins. Yet it seems more or less certain that something like poker was played in French Louisiana and that it spread to the United States around 1800 and to England afterward. Because of the imitation of English habits, games, and clothes characteristic of much of Europe's aristocracy and upper bourgeoisie in the nineteenth century, poker made its way across the Continent; indeed, it was (and still is) one of the few American things that most Europeans erroneously attribute to England. From scattered bits of information, including literature and memoirs and personal reminiscences of older people, I can say that poker was mildly fashionable among the Orleanist aristocracy of France in the 1860's; it was played in Turin around 1865; it arrived in Vienna in the 1870's, in Hungary in the 1880's, in Russia around 1900. By about 1920 poker, with other formerly aristocratic habits and pastimes, filtered down to the level of the bourgeoisie, which is where I became acquainted with it in 1938, at the age of fifteen, in my native Hungary.

The uniqueness of poker consists in its being a game of chance where the element of chance itself is subordinated to psychological factors and where it is not so much fate as human beings who decide. In this respect poker is the game closest to the Western conception of life, where life and thought are recognized as intimately combined, where free will prevails over philosophies of fate or of chance, where men are considered free moral agents, and where—at least in the short run—the important thing is not what happens but what people think happens.

To some extent, of course, this element is present in a number of sophisticated games of chance in which bluffing, or the character of the player, may become decisive on crucial occasions. But in the playing of poker this factor is not occasional but constant, not secondary but primary. Like certain other games of chance, poker is played not primarily with cards but with money; unlike other games, the money staked in poker represents not only our idea of the value of our cards, but our idea of what the other players' idea of the value of our cards might be.

All other unique characteristics of poker flow from this condition. Thus, in the second place, cards count in poker, but they count less than in any other game. There are good players and bad players in every game: there are, contrary to the supercilious belief of mathematicians, even such things as good and bad roulette players. But even in such an intelligent game as bridge a bad player is almost sure

of ending up in the black if, by chance, he has a succession of very good hands all evening. Conversely, the good poker player—like the good artist or the fine *viveur*—may make much out of little on the one hand and, on the other, limit his losses by strict self-discipline.

In the third place, poker—again unlike other games—becomes gradually more interesting the more one plays with the same group of people (provided, of course, they are agreeable partners). Since the important thing is not the cards but the betting, not the value of the player's hand but the player's psychology, as one gets to know the habits, the quirks, the tendencies, the strengths, and the weaknesses of the other players—which, more than often, are reflections of character strengths and weaknesses—the play becomes increasingly interesting. Whereas in bridge there is a certain social charm in getting acquainted with previously unknown partners at a resort hotel, a poker game between four or five characters unknown to each other must, by necessity, be stiff, angular, and unduly cautious—except for the professional cardsharp, of course.

The reason for this is that in poker you play not against chance or fate but against people, human beings; and what is important about them is not so much how they play their cards but how they bet their money. There is, thus, in the game of poker—perhaps alone among games of chance—a unique element of reality. This reality—which is the fourth characteristic of the game—derives from the condition that you must play within your means. Money is the basis of poker: whereas bridge can be played for fun without money, poker becomes utterly senseless if played without it. Note that I said *money*, not *chips*—chips only when they represent money and money only because it represents the daring or the cowardice of other people. Poker, to repeat, can be played only with people and, unlike chess or even bridge, never against an IBM machine.* On the other end of the scale, poker again becomes senseless if the people who play it have too much money—to

---

*A relatively simple mathematical computation will show some of the following probabilities out of the 2,598,960 possible hands of classic draw poker played with the standard fifty-two-card deck:

Flush	5,108	(or once in 509 hands)
Straight	10,200	(or once in 256 hands)
Three of a kind	54,912	(or once in 48 hands)
Two Pairs	123,552	(or once in 21 hands)
One Pair	1,098,240	(or once in $2\frac{1}{2}$ hands)
Other hands	1,302,540	(or once in 2 hands)

I reproduce these figures from John McDonald's *Strategy in Poker, Business, and War*, a book to which I shall return. Yet every poker player will, I think, feel that at closer scrutiny there is something strange about them. It just does not happen that, on the average, one has to wait 48 hands for three of a kind, or 256 hands for a straight. And, besides, what are $2\frac{1}{2}$ hands?

give a concrete example, if people of, say, $30,000-a-year incomes sit down to play with chips representing nothing higher than pennies. This, of course, is true of other games, too—but only to some extent. Clearly the very rich person, whether at the gin-rummy table or at the horse races, has a certain advantage over others: he can take chances which other players cannot, but he can also lose more—and that rich people gamble more successfully than poor ones is yet to be demonstrated. This is not so in poker, where a group of people with moderate incomes cannot afford to play regularly with a happy-go-lucky millionaire, whose attitude toward money will be different; and this is what counts in the end.

For, in the end, poker is also a game of a thousand unwritten rules. It is a game for gentlemen, and for gentlemen alone; and by this I do not mean that it requires social class but only those unwritten and often hardly conscious social standards and codes of behavior that constitute the subsoil of certain historical cultures. I cannot imagine Syrians or Burmese, including aristocrats or philosophers, playing poker in the way it was played in English or American clubs around 1880. This is not what sociologists call a value judgment: it is a historical condition. It has little to do with the rules of the game. Except for the dealing practices of the cardsharp, it is difficult to cheat in poker, but this is not the point. The point is that there are a thousand different ways in which poker can be played *legally* but *not quite correctly*, where its rules are strictly observed but its human relationships are not. People play poker in the way they want to play it; it is a game based to a large extent on free will, a game that flows from the necessity that we recognize a certain relationship between image and reality and that, for the sake of the game, this relationship be kept reasonably proportionate—an eminently Western game.

Poker, as played in Hungary during the years when I first learned the game, reflected something of the Hungarian national character. It was classic draw poker but with one important variation: the lower cards were excluded from the deck. Thus, for example, in a game of four (the minimum for a poker table) the lowest cards were sevens; when five persons played, the sixes were left in the deck; when seven were playing (the reasonable maximum), the fives were added. This kind of playing with a thirty-six- or forty-card deck did make the game quicker and perhaps more exciting: there were more good hands, and the hierarchy of hands was slightly changed. This lent the game a certain

jaded but very Hungarian grandiloquence and *brio*. On the other hand, there was a slight but appreciable class difference between the several varieties of the game: certain people played with a gin-rummy deck, including the two Jolly Jokers which were naturally wild. "To play poker with a joker," I once heard my mother superciliously observe, "is a lower-class game."

All of my family were Anglophiles: indeed, my mother Anglomaniacally so. I remember the profound expression of shock on her face when two German visitors, business acquaintances of my stepfather, assured her in 1943 that many Germans, especially in Hamburg, played poker too; her incredulity was only partly assuaged by the subsequent assurance that those were anti-Nazis. It was around that time, during what had become the ritual practice of listening to London short-wave broadcasts over a large Telefunken radio, that we heard a human-interest background report about General Eisenhower: among other things, we were informed that he liked to play poker for relaxation. This piece of precious intelligence about the new Supreme Allied Commander filled us with great joy and hope. A poker-playing American general, we agreed, would be a general with nonchalance and dash and that loose-limbed, easygoing, natural elegance of action characteristic of Americans: this was the image that rose before us immediately; he would give short shrift to the methodical Germans.

This was before the invasion of Sicily. Our hopes were to be disappointed; the Italian front, the one closest to Hungary, bogged down in a largely senseless campaign. It took Eisenhower nearly a year to get from Naples to Rome, then another year from Normandy to Berlin. By that time the Russians, not the Anglo-Americans, had conquered Hungary, a bloody and prostrate country mostly in ruins, where no more poker was to be played for a long, long time. Not until eight or nine years later, during the Presidential campaign of 1952, did I learn that while Truman was a poker-playing President (and a President, too, with a great deal of historical sense), Eisenhower was not a poker player but a bridge addict.

I had many illusions about the United States when I landed in Portland, Maine, on a converted troopship in October, 1946. These illusions included poker. I was coming, I told myself, to the fatherland of poker, to the classic country of poker, where everybody plays poker, where I would have unlimited opportunities to amuse myself during the long American weekends. I understood that the American public was saturated with knowledge of the game and even "absorbed its language," as John McDonald put it; "every American, poker player or not, knows what it is to have an ace in the hole (or up the sleeve) or to be in the chips, to bluff or call a bluff, stand pat, four-flush, put his cards on the table, have a showdown, or otherwise get into a situation where the chips are down; and finally to meet the end of life itself by cashing in the chips."

I have now lived in the United States for seventeen years; and I have played less poker here than during an average month in Hungary. Some of this undoubtedly has been the consequence of the strenuous quality of American life: I have certainly had less time (and, strangely enough, also less money) for poker playing than in Hungary. The main reason, however, is that the overwhelming majority of my friends now play a game that is still called poker, but its relationship to poker is about as distant as that of General Lee's horse, Traveller, to Eisenhower's bubble-top limousine—no, to his electric golf-cart. In seventeen years I have been able to organize a classic, or draw, poker game but once. At best, I have been able to compromise, on a one-sixth or one-seventh basis, meaning that when we play dealer's choice, I choose five-card draw on my turn.

I must now explain, in brief, the differences between classic (or draw) poker on the one hand, and *all* other variations of poker on the other. In *every* other variation of poker—from the mildest (one card wild) to the wildest (seven-card stud, high-low)—the human factor is weakened and the factor of chance is correspondingly increased; seven-card stud resembles a gambling game with poker nomenclature but not very different from flipping seven pennies and betting on them in turn. In these games the unique character of poker is damaged, and perhaps ultimately destroyed. I need not enumerate here the many variations of the game—"baseball" or "spit-in-the-ocean," for example—that are widely and extravagantly played in America today. My point is that these "improvements" fatally affect the character of the game, so that it would be perhaps proper and just not to call them poker at all.

The most important of these fundamental changes is the considerable reduction of the unique poker opportunity of bluffing. Thereby the four essential characteristics of poker, mentioned earlier, no longer exist. It becomes a gambling game, with a few conventional variations remaining; it is a contest not between human personalities who represent themselves through money and cards, but between cards held fortuitously by certain individuals.

What has happened?

It is very difficult to know anything definite about the historical development of the game. It is, however, ascer-tainable that by about 1840 poker was widespread in western America. It seems, too, that this was the time when most of the present rules of draw poker grew up, and they were apparently well established before the Civil War. There is a story according to which the game was introduced in England when the American Minister showed it to Queen Victoria in 1872, but even though the latter event seems authentic, much evidence indicates that poker was played in England as early as 1850. During the nineteenth century the majority of English and American enthusiasts stuck to straight draw; the wilder variations of the game were to be found in mining camps, on the frontier and, according to certain legends, among Negroes in New Orleans, whence poker, like jazz, was supposed to have gone up the Mississippi.

Draw poker was therefore an American or, at the very least, an Anglo-American game. Indeed, it seems that an American innovation gave the game its definite shape as early as a century and a half ago; before that time the Louisiana French had played *poque* with a smaller deck, and with hands of three or four cards each. The introduction of the fifty-two-card deck gave poker a more masculine character, making it what I call a "low-scoring game." In this I tend to see a certain reflection of the characteristics of an Anglo-Saxon and democratic people, since one could win with relatively low cards, without the ubiquitous hierarchical royalty of kings, queens, and knaves. (Thus the face cards became less influential but more rare—as in nineteenth-century England the political influence of royalty lessened but its social influence rose.)

The golden age of poker in the United States seems to have been from 1870 to 1920. It seems, too, that contrary to the general assumption poker was not played mainly on the frontier and was not considered an archetypal gambling game. Poker, in those decades, was often an American drawing-room game, a game played in law offices after hours, a game for men, a game played by small-town friends in thousands of parlors from Maryland to Missouri, a manly and somewhat raffish pastime but one with a solid mahogany core, with a certain late-Victorian tinge. There is no doubt that the wilder variations of the game were already widespread by 1900; but from what I know of its intra-American history, the practice of draw poker began to fade rapidly only after the First World War, and to vanish from large areas during the Second, so that in 1946, by the time I arrived in the United States, it was already something of a rarity.

When certain people tend to act in certain ways, they also tend—note again that I say tend, not will—to play in certain ways. I believe, for example, that the social acceptance of poker-playing women may well have had a bad effect on the game. This began around 1920, after the Constitutional amendment ordering female suffrage and around the time when smoking by women began to be generally accepted. I believe that this wide introduction of the female element diluted the character of poker (just as Prohibition led, however indirectly, to the dilution of table spirits). Women are notoriously bad gamblers; they find it difficult to exclude social considerations from a game that must be organized around a social occasion; whereas in bridge, an intellectual and calculating game, women are equals and often superiors of men, this is not true of poker, with its strongly masculine characteristics.

Another bad influence was the frequency of gambling, under deleterious conditions, among servicemen and officers during the Second World War. These soldiers were playing poker day after day, for exorbitant sums, when they had nothing else to do. To play poker out of boredom will eventually lead to a deterioration of the game: the longer the boredom, the more artificial the excitements demanded by the human spirit. Consequently, during the war years hundreds of thousands of young Americans were introduced to a kind of poker in which "anything went" and wild games abounded, for the earlier mentioned subtle but very important relationship between the players and their normal financial circumstances was missing—in the shadow of possible death and amid the irregular interruptions of Army life, money could not possibly have the same meaning as in times of peace.

Since poker is still probably the most widespread domestic gambling game in America, and since poker playing and the poker player have become accepted and respectable prototypes of American behavior, many young people, from bored interns to the sons of clergymen, craving group acceptance and social sophistication, have chosen to learn and play poker at some time during their early years, even though many of them may have been characteristically or temperamentally better suited to other games of chance. The result of all this, and of many other things besides, is the present degeneration of poker into a game of chance with some of the original vocabulary and framework left to maintain the name of poker—in my opinion, fraudulently so.

In this development I see reflected the erosion of the American national character. The deterioration of poker, I believe, corresponds very closely to a tendency in modern American life that I find most disturbing and dangerous: the inflation (meaning the increasing worthlessness) of words—more menacing, even, than the inflation of money. Seven-card stud poker represents a gross inflation of values. It corresponds to the development of a society where everybody goes to college until the value of the college degree is less than that of a high-school degree forty years ago; where everybody nominally owns a house but with less sense of permanence and of privacy than the owner of a family flat in a Naples tenement; where the Great American Novel of The Generation is published at least twice, and of Our Decade at least five times, a year; and where everybody calls everybody else by his first name. Depending on cards rather than on one's own judgment reflects, too, a deterioration of self-confidence: in this respect the new kind of poker suggests some of the habits of the Organization Man. It also represents a form of immaturity, a strange kind of grown-up disorderliness covering up what is fundamentally an adolescent attitude.

Through seven-card stud and other wild games, poker has been transformed from a low-scoring to a high-scoring game. In this respect it resembles basketball, a sport I abhor, since I cannot find much interest in a game where scores run 158–142, where even the worst team will make forty or fifty points, and where the gangling six-foot-eight-inch player is the inevitable joker, the wild card in the deck. Seven-card stud and its cousins are also truly Alice-in-Wonderland games of egalitarian democracy, where flushes are as frequent as two pairs in the older draw poker, where everybody wins and therefore nobody wins. In the large-scale limitation on bluffing it is perhaps not going too far to detect a craving for security or perhaps even for the welfare state. Just as those American businessmen who so often cry out against the passing of free enterprise have, through conformity and overorganization, helped to bring about the bureaucratization of business, so the addicts of wild and unruly poker are really conformists at heart. They have grossly exaggerated the element of blind fate; they have weakened the element of self-reliance in what was once a great American game.

A word remains to be said about the crowning absurdity of what has happened to poker: its study in our government-supported research institutes in universities and by our armed services as a science, under the idiotic name of Games Theory. It is difficult for me not to be abusive: for this development is part and parcel of the recent inclination of generals and admirals to listen in awe to the theories of our military intellectuals, usually refugee economists of Central European origin, who more than often cannot tell a shotgun from a rifle. It all began during World War II, this relatively recent American passion—so utterly unlike the Anglo-American past—for intellectualizing everything, from business to military strategy. Thus, while on the one hand the playing of poker becomes perverted, on the other hand poker is given an elaborate theory and becomes an object of scientific study—insufficient seriousness on one end, overseriousness on the other.

The "scientification" of poker has come about in two ways. First, mathematicians and nuclear scholars were for some time compelled to pay increasing attention to theories of probability (because of the collapse of earlier scientific assumptions about absolute mathematical certainty, but that is another story). Consequently some of them tried to examine and to illustrate probability theories through games of chance. The most notable result was a book by two Princeton luminaries, Oskar Morgenstern and the late John von Neumann, called *Theory of Games and Economic Behavior*, which around 1945 stirred the scholarly world to its depths. (It is perhaps symptomatic that during the following decade one of these eminent Central European savants, an erstwhile mathematician, became a hydrogen-bomb chief; the other, an erstwhile economist, a leading war theorist.) In 1948 John Mc-Donald, a writer for *Fortune*, was sufficiently impressed by the book's reputation to consider expanding his excellent article "Poker, An American Game" into a more philosophical volume entitled *Strategy in Poker, Business, and War*. Subsequently, as his acknowledgment reads, McDonald felt compelled to consult not only professors Von Neumann and Morgenstern of Princeton but professors Ernest Nagel of Columbia, J. K. Galbraith of Harvard, John W. Tukey (again of Princeton), E. J. Gumbel of the New School for Social Research, Herbert A. Simon of the Illinois Institute of Technology, Jacob Marschak of the Cowles Commission, University of Chicago; Dr. E. W. Paxson of the Rand Corporation; Dr. Gunnar Boe, former Norwegian representative to the United Nations Economic and Employment Commission; and W. Edward Deming of the U.S. Bureau of the Budget. The result was a book whose chapter on poker, written by its author without the benefit of extensive scholarly consultations, is sensible and witty; and the rest of which is either nonsense or else, as Oscar Wilde would have said, pursues the obvious with

the enthusiasm of a shortsighted detective. I cannot, at this point, go into metaphysical and philosophical details about how and why mathematical Games Theory has (or, rather, should have) nothing to do with poker. I have already said that poker is a game which cannot be played against an IBM machine; I must content myself with drawing attention to two principal assumptions of the games theorists. The first assumption—a mathematical *sine qua non*—is, of course, that all players are of the same temperament: an inhuman or nonhuman condition that cannot be found in reality. The second, and perhaps centrally important, assumption of the professorial gamesters represents the crystallization of their arguments. "Like all economic theories," (harrumph!) "the theory of games," McDonald writes, "is based on the assumption that man seeks gain." I have yet to see the man, except for the professional cardsharp, who plays poker because he primarily seeks gain. He plays for fun; and he hopes to make some gain. (Not the reverse. *Homo ludens*; not *homo faber*.)

By 1947 the armed services had given Games Theory a high security classification which, as McDonald put it in 1950, "is a sign that its intent is anything but trifling. A young scientist attached to the Air Force said . . . of its military application, 'We hope it will work, just as we hoped in 1942 that the atomic bomb would work.'" It certainly did. The result is with us, in the seven-hundred- to one-thousand-page volumes of our eminent warrior intellectuals, Professors Kissinger, Kahn, Morgenthau, and Morgenstern, each dealing with missiles, communism, Russia, the moon, hydrogen, war, peace, life, death. It is anything but trifling.

By the end of the fifties the books and articles of the games and military theorists amounted to several hundred, while the editors of American military journals set out on a quest to acquire the brilliant writings of military intellectuals for their professional warrior readership. Finally, as a result, we have reached the logical dead end of this development: a call for banishing the poker mentality from American thinking.

Spurred in part by the great Sputnik Panic of 1957, numerous professors, congressmen, and anti-communist experts have now drawn attention to the important role that chess, together with Marxism, plays in the Russian educational system. An example of this argument appeared in the May, 1962, issue of the *United States Naval Institute Proceedings*, a venerable maritime monthly, originally devoted to problems of naval history and seamanship, but lately more and more concerned with such profound matters as Ideology, Programming, Operational Research. In an article entitled "Contrasting Strategic Styles in the Cold War," which received honorable mention in the annual prize-essay contest of the United States Naval Institute, the author, Professor Charles O. Lerche, announced that "probably the most basic difference in strategic style between the Soviet Union and the United States is dramatically suggested by the Russian preference for chess as an intellectual pastime in contrast to the American predilection for either poker or contract bridge."

"American behavior in the Cold War," according to the author, who teaches international relations at American University, "is rooted—possibly unwittingly—in the bridge-poker school of strategy." This is a grave shortcoming, we are given to understand, since the essence of strategy in chess "is in its integral unity. The entire plan of attack is tied together from the very first move. . . . In chess, victory (checkmate) is won by one move made *at the end of the game*." "The crisis of decision facing the United States at this point in history," Lerche says, repeating an argument that has been made by now not only by our military intellectuals but also by new conservatives and psychological-warfare experts, "is whether the nation can safely go on playing poker with a chess master. . . . Under the conditions of military and political technology in the latter half of the twentieth century, what chance has a strategy of opportunity against a strategy of finality?" The answer, in my opinion, is: Lots.

Poker is a unique game because it approximates life. This is not true of chess, which is circumscribed by a framework of mathematical rules and is therefore irrevocably artificial. Even though the variations of its calculations are almost infinite, the rules are inflexible. That is why there are so many chess players of the rank of genius who are no good at anything else: their extraordinary capacity for mental gymnastics, on the one hand, being offset, on the other, by a generally below-average allowance of common sense (the theme of the late Stefan Zweig's *Royal Game*). Similarly, a thorough knowledge of Marxist epistemology gave precious little help to the Russian generals who faced German Panzer divisions in 1941. I do not remember having read that Stalin was a chess player (but, then, he probably read very little Marx either). Clausewitz —from whom Lenin learned more than from Marx—is not recorded as having been a chess addict, but he knew an estimable amount of history.

"The chess strategist," writes Lerche, "has a major ad-

vantage over the poker player . . . he has a broader strategic outlook and many more analytical criteria." The very opposite is true—fortunately and, also, alas. Alas, because the widespread and fashionable nature of the chess-above-poker argument is, in itself, a symptom of American over-intellectualization, of the fatal departure from earlier American habits and traditions: God save the nation that prepares its young officers for war by making them play chess against business machines. Fortunately, because I believe that the common sense of Americans will in the end assert itself, as befits a nation of erstwhile poker—*draw* poker—players.

I have nothing against chess. I wish the Russians luck with it. It is a game typical of the concentrated and mathematical turn of mind; its character somewhat corresponds to the ironclad (and already greatly superseded) categorical thinking of dogmatic Marxists. Logical, rational, scientific as it then seemed, Marxism represented to certain Russians the very intellectual antithesis to the fatalistic, mystical, irrational inclinations of the Russian character— manifest, for example, in the Russian penchant for mad gambling, described profoundly and inimitably by Dostoevsky in *The Gambler* (his most honest, since most autobiographical, book). For the compulsive gambler the play elements in any game are subordinated to pure chance— as in Russian roulette, which carries to a logical extreme man's challenge to fate—an attitude perhaps not untypical of a people with an Oriental streak in their history and character. It was in resistance to this kind of Byzantine and Oriental fatalism that certain Russian intellectuals turned to the idea that life could be ordered and arranged as a logical and mathematical proposition—with results that are (or, rather, should be) painfully obvious. But life and love and poker and war are not mathematical propositions; indeed, life is stronger than theory—which is just what the nonintellectual genius of the English-speaking peoples has intuitively recognized, and which has been the source of their historical greatness. "The key point," according to Lerche, is that "the conditions under which strategic choices are made are radically different in chess than in the games favored by Americans."

You bet.

Mr. Lukacs, a historian, teaches at Chestnut and LaSalle Colleges, Philadelphia, and is author of A History of the Cold War *and the forthcoming* Historical Thinking.

THE ENIGMATIC URN

By NEIL McKENDRICK

During the artistic rape of Europe in the eighteenth century—the ransack that is now known as the Grand Tour—England was flooded with cultural spoils of her wandering noblemen. Paintings, porcelain and pottery, sculpture, jewelry, and tapestry poured into the country in an ill-sorted, ill-chosen mass. Much was fake, much was commonplace, but occasionally pieces of unparalleled beauty or fame were acquired. Of these, few can compare with the Barberini vase.

It stands now in the British Museum—a small, heavily cracked vase made of nothing more remarkable or valuable than glass. Many consider its shape undistinguished, others find its decoration uninspired, and no one can deny that it is no longer perfect. Yet it is, perhaps, the most famous vase in the world.

Its early history has never been satisfactorily explained. Sir William Hamilton was certain that it was a work of the fourth century B.C., carried in triumph out of Asia by Alexander the Great to bear his ashes when he died; others thought that it was the burial urn of the Roman emperor Alexander Severus and his mother, Mamaea, who were murdered by the Roman legions in Germany some six hundred years later; and during the eighteenth and nineteenth centuries almost everybody believed that it had been buried—complete with somebody's ashes—and was not revealed again until 1582, when it was said to have been found in a sarcophagus dug from Monte del Grano.

But intriguing as these beliefs are, they are almost certainly untrue. This is a great pity, because without them it is impossible to explain the whereabouts of the vase, from its creation in the hands of a pre-Christian glassmaker in Alexandria to its reappearance some seventeen hundred years later in the possession of the famous Barberini family in Rome. Wherever it had wandered over the centuries, they were determined that it should wander no more. In fact, so proud of the vase was the Barberini pope, Urban VIII, that he gave specific instructions that this gem of the family collection should never leave Rome.

Unhappily, he had reckoned without the eighteenth century's addiction to gambling. In an age when betting played as large a part in social life as hunting and dancing, it is not surprising that even Princess Barberini should occasionally have difficulties in meeting her debts. She sold the pot to pay them; but not unnaturally, considering the papal ban, she sold it in secret, and there is little record of the transaction.

Princess Barberini sold it to James Byres, a Scottish antiquary who lived in Rome and supplemented his income by helping *milords inglesi* find suitable trophies to take back to England at the end of their Grand Tour. It was not in his hands for long. He showed it to Sir William Hamilton, who, according to his own records, promptly bought it for £1,000.

Sir William, who is mostly remembered now as the husband of Emma Hamilton, Nelson's mistress, was then well known as an enthusiastic connoisseur and one of the first to popularize the discoveries at Herculaneum as part of the Grand Tour. It was he who brought the vase into England in 1784.

Who made it? What is its secret? And through how many hands had it passed before it came into these?

POPE URBAN VIII
He wanted to keep it

SIR WILLIAM HAMILTON
He made a profit on it

JOSIAH WEDGWOOD
He reproduced it

LADY PORTLAND
She hid it

ALEXANDER THE GREAT
He wasn't in it

Its fame had preceded it, and Sir William was bombarded with notes, letters, and secret messages from the art-crazed Lady Portland, an avid collector of the rare or the unique. She paid him 1,800 guineas for it (roughly equivalent to $56,000 by present-day values), but once in her hands, the Barberini disappeared from view. In fact, she had conducted the whole transaction "with such secrecy," according to Josiah Wedgwood, "that she was never known, even by her own family, to be the possessor of it." The secrecy is easily explained. Lady Portland's family had become alarmed at her eccentric buying, and she clearly did not wish them to hear of her latest extravagance.

To Wedgwood, the disappearance of the vase was maddening. He was planning, as a final test of his technical skill, to produce a copy, and he had only drawings to work from. But Lady Portland, like an ecstatic squirrel with a unique nut, had secreted it away among her most precious possessions and would show it to none but her closest friends. Within a year, however, she was dead, and within three days of the auction of her collection, the vase was in Wedgwood's hands. The third Duke of Portland had bought it back into the family for 980 guineas and promptly lent it to England's leading potter for reproduction.

Within the next century it was reproduced in plaster, glass, brass, silver, iron, marble, and even in wood. But by far the most famous and most perfect copies were those made in jasper by Josiah Wedgwood in the early 1790's. People clamored for copies, but such were the difficulties of production that they were never a commercial proposition, and today they are so rare that they have fetched up to $1,344 in the sale room. It was felt to be a triumph for Wedgwood and a triumph for English pottery. In the words of Wolf Mankowitz, the vase's latest and most reliable historian, it was "the most refined work—so the age felt—ever accomplished in European ceramic history."

It has been reproduced by others ever since, but never with the same success. Even the later attempts of the Wedgwood firm could not compare with the efforts of the first Josiah. Their 1839 version was of much poorer quality. In fact, it is more of a landmark in Victorian morality than in the history of pottery, for the charming little cupid was made to cross his legs to hide his embryonic manhood, and the other figures, naked and unashamed in the original, were draped with a thoroughness that would have satisfied Victoria herself.

Conjecture about the vase did not decline, but the chief interest was now directed to interpreting the story it depicts. On one side a girl is caressing a serpent with one hand and reaching up with the other to welcome a young man who is wearing nothing but a hesitant air. A plump cupid hovers above, and an older bearded man looks thoughtfully on. On the other side two young women lie in negligent undress beneath a tree as a handsome youth looks longingly toward them. To add a further complication, a robed figure holding a finger to his lips is carved on the base. Such material can be made to fit a host of mythological stories.

At first the vase was assumed to be the burial urn of Marcus Aurelius Antoninus and his wife, Faustina, and the story that of the famous physician Galen diagnosing their daughter's mysterious illness as love for a ropedancer. Certainly this interpretation can be made to fit the figures on the vase (though what part the serpent played is difficult to understand), and the daughter's known taste for muscular young men such as wrestlers, ropedancers, and gladiators supports it; unfortunately, the likelihood of a Roman emperor decorating his burial urn with the story of his daughter's casual love affairs is extremely remote.

The other interpretations are a similar mixture of the plausible and the absurd. With minor adjustments, the figures have been made to fit the love stories of Medea and Jason, Theseus and Amphitrite, Jupiter and Olympias, or Zeus and Leda (in which case the serpent would have to be a swan). To Erasmus Darwin, refreshingly but implausibly, the figures suggested a fertility cult from Asia Minor; if so, the male figure must have been the most reluctant hero in the history of fertility rites.

To these suggestions there were constant additions. But in the middle of the nineteenth century the vase was thrust far more dramatically before the public eye. For on Friday, February 7, 1845, William Lloyd secured his only niche in history when he stepped from a crowd of spectators in the British Museum and hurled a stone sculpture through the only perfect surviving example of Greek cameo glass. It was not a premeditated act, not the act of a madman. He simply felt a sudden uncheckable desire to smash something, and the most famous vase in the world happened to be the handiest and most tempting target in sight.

Now, carefully pieced together again, it stands unostentatiously in the British Museum. Probably few of those who stop to look realize the mysteries that still surround it. But whatever the possibilities of its strange career, they can be little more remarkable than the certainties. And what happened to it during its first seventeen hundred years of existence, we shall never know for certain. Like the story told by the vase, it is open to speculation.

Earlier (and related) articles by Neil McKendrick were "Wedgwood and His Friends" in HORIZON *for May, 1959, and "Pompeii" in the issue of March, 1962. He is a lecturer in history at Cambridge.*

SHAPES FROM THE ANCIENT

These gnarled and blunted figures—at first glance not too different from the lumps of mud or stone from which they were fashioned —could never be mistaken for prehistoric toys or crude attempts at portraiture. Their concentrated power and stillness tell us clearly that we are in the presence of the gods. Made by unknown hands some eight to nine thousand years ago, they may not be the world's first religious sculptures—but they are the earliest that have yet been found.

They were discovered last year by the English archaeologist James Mellaart * at Çatal Hüyük, an ancient mound of rubbish in southern Turkey that contains the remains of ten neolithic cities, one above another like the layers of a cake. Çatal Hüyük has already yielded some astonishing murals, but the sculptures were found at a lower and thus earlier level. This level shows signs of a terrific conflagration that evidently destroyed the settlement circa 6500 B.C., so the figures are at least as old as that. But some must be a great deal older: they are scarred or worn in a way that suggests they were heirlooms from an earlier age.

The figures are of two kinds. There is a group of crudely schematic renderings in clay of men and animals—ex-votos, no doubt, or magic talismans; the animals may be substitutes for actual offerings, the human beings the donors. More remarkable are the carved figures of marble or limestone, found on the floor of what was unmistakably a shrine. Among them was an almost wholly natural shape, probably the broken-off end of a stalactite, on which a head and features had been carved. Is this the beginning of sculpture? Others are little more than limestone pebbles with suggestive shapes, such as that of a pregnant woman, to which incised mouth, eyes, and ears were added. But the best of them are like the figure at left—strongly carved and extraordinarily expressive.

All of the figures represent elements of a fertility cult, and in a way they sum up what we know about neolithic man's beliefs. His chief concern was with sustaining and increasing his food supply, and so the chief deity in his pantheon was the Great Mother—source of all life, creator and destroyer, mistress of death and resurrection. When she herself was born in man's mind we do not know, but some clues may lie still farther down in the inexhaustible mound of Çatal Hüyük.

* See "Man's First Murals" by James Mellaart, HORIZON, September, 1962.

Among the oldest statues in the world,

these recently discovered figures

from Anatolia show something of the

prime impulses that gave rise to art

The grim old mother goddess on the page oppo-site dominated Çatal Hüyük's mythology. Her son appeared in both animal form, symbolized by the bull's heads shown at the top of the same page, and in human form, as pictured on this page at bottom left. Moving clockwise, the hu-man figure with a group of animals represents both sacrificer and sacrificed in religious rites; the headless daughter goddess is shown as "Mis-tress of Animals" with her spotted leopard; and some semblance of family unity is brought to these fragments of mythology by the twin goddesses—mother and daughter together. At bottom center is a group of clay figures, per-haps the first lady's divine attendants. But we do not know the name of the goddess, any more than we know the name of the people— or race—who lived so long ago at Çatal Hüyük.

ARTH

The Çatal Hüyük excavations, under the direction of James Mellaart, are supported by the Bollingen and Wenner-Gren foundations of New York; the British Academy; the Australian Institute of Ar-chaeology; the universities of Edinburgh and of Canterbury, N.Z. Photographs by Mrs. Mellaart.

From "Bully!"

The style is the same—inherited wealth, Cuba, exuberance,

Harvard, rocking chair, and all—but there are profound

differences, as well as similarities, between T.R. and J.F.K.

It is becoming a parlor game in Washington to compare the present very active regime in the White House with that of Theodore Roosevelt, who was the most active of all our presidents, by far. Also, quite aside from athletics, there are some remarkable similarities between J.F.K. and T.R. Each, for example, was a rich man's son, a Harvardman, a historian; each worked on his first book while still an undergraduate. And each advanced in public life on his repute as a war hero.

Both, as youngsters, were somewhat frail. J.F.K. had recurrent jaundice and, in order to play football, forced himself to gain thirty pounds. Like T.R. before him, Kennedy went West for his health. His best sport was swimming. During World War II in the Pacific, his endurance, courage, and skill in the water saved his own life, and that of some of his men, after the sinking of their PT boat. Widely distributed reprints of a magazine article about this episode, in 1946, helped to elect him to Congress. And since his career moved forward thereafter in a straight line, it can be said that Jack Kennedy swam into the White House.

Teddy Roosevelt, of course, rode in on horseback—a national hero after he led the Rough Riders up San Juan Hill. On his Western ranch young Teddy had made friends with the cowboys from whom—with a sprinkling of Ivy Leaguers —he formed his famous cavalry regiment. Actually, they had fought dismounted in Cuba, but the horseback image stuck, and when he campaigned for governor of New York after the Spanish-American War, T.R. took pains to display Rough Riders in their characteristic costume (and to have the band play "There'll Be a Hot Time in the Old Town Tonight"). Two years later, with the death of McKinley, he was in the White House.

Reminders of T.R.'s administration have been cropping up ever since J.F.K.'s inauguration—almost to the point where Mr. Kennedy, himself a student of Teddy Roosevelt, may feel that he is living another man's life over again.

The Roosevelts, for example—succeeding a rather stodgy, business-minded regime—promptly redecorated the White House and made it a center for artists and writers, as it had never been before. Passers-by stopped, as they do today, to peer through the fence hoping to catch a glimpse of the Presidential children, who were called "The White House Gang." (*Their* pony even rode the White House elevators.) And just as a crowd of Kennedys seems always to surround our own President, especially at his summer home, so the numerous tribe of Roosevelts swarmed to T.R.'s home at Oyster Bay, Long Island. (His favorite niece, Eleanor Roosevelt, remembered that one day in order to avoid being thrown in the water by her uncle she leaped in, fully clothed.)

J.F.K. sent his beautiful and charming wife on a goodwill tour of Asia; T.R. dispatched his beautiful and charming daughter Alice, and her tour produced much the same sort of headlines. One of these concerned an occasion when she leaped into a swimming pool with *her* clothes on—a form of recreation which fairly seems to haunt White House activists in each generation. A friend of the Kennedys once wrote that if one went to luncheon there, touch football afterward was unavoidable, cautioning that it was not only necessary to play but highly advisable to display "raw guts." In accepting an invitation from the Theodore Roosevelts it was even more necessary to be ready for anything. The President was apt to suggest a walk after luncheon, and Teddy Roosevelt's walks make the Kennedys' football seem like croquet.

T.R. was a point-to-point walker. The rule was never to avoid any obstacle but to proceed in a straight line, even if

to "Vigah!"

By ARCHIE ROBERTSON

it meant climbing a barn or cliff, or swimming an icy, raging stream. An Army officer in line for promotion who could not keep up with his Commander-in-chief on a walk was very likely to be disappointed in his hopes. One sedentary general who lost his glasses scrambling down a steep bank and floundered helpless at the bottom was escorted grimly by the President to the nearest park policeman. "Take this officer to the streetcar line," said T.R., "and remember, he's a general of the United States Army."

T.R. not only suggested the fifty-mile hike for infantry, which J.F.K. has made fashionable once more, but the hundred-mile ride for cavalry officers—and to prove his point, while in his fifties he slipped away from the secret service one winter day to ride ninety-eight miles over the frozen Virginia roads. He liked to test the mettle of foreign diplomats, too. When he led a group of luncheon guests to the banks of the old canal in Georgetown, most followed his example and plunged in fully clothed. But the French ambassador insisted on removing all his clothes—except his gloves. "Because I thought we might meet ladies," he explained.

The strenuous life of Theodore Roosevelt even extended to his rocking chair. (In the course of a warm argument it would slide vehemently all the way across the room.) It also involved his wife, naturally. Just as Mrs. Jacqueline Kennedy has broken an ankle at the family's touch football, so Mrs. Edith Roosevelt, galloping near Oyster Bay with T.R., fell and suffered a severe head injury. Most of the time, however, Edith Roosevelt managed to maintain a remarkable atmosphere of order and calm. She was not at all afraid of her rambunctious husband. When he came in at Oyster Bay after a bruising and abrading fall from a windmill, she said only:

"Theodore, I do wish you'd do your bleeding in the bathroom. You're spoiling every rug in the house."

The social sympathies of the two men, Republican and Democrat, have an innate resemblance—perhaps because each grew up in middle-class comfort only to have his eyes opened with startling suddenness to the sight of the poor. T.R., then serving as New York City police commissioner, was astounded when Jacob Riis, author of *How the Other Half Lives,* took him on an extended tour of the slums. Kennedy, according to his biographer James McGregor Burns, was similarly shocked when he first campaigned for Congress among "the drab and noisome tenements in Charlestown and East Boston." In his first congressional term he fought the real-estate lobby, the American Legion, and the late Senator Joe McCarthy on behalf of slum-clearance legislation. (In the Senate, it will be remembered, the battle was led by the conservative Republican Robert A. Taft.) Kennedy did not then, nor does he now, consider himself a "liberal." He simply believed that as a matter of decency something had to be done.

This was basically T.R.'s attitude, too, in advancing such radical proposals as unemployment insurance, workmen's compensation, health insurance in industry, and the abolition of child labor. He was completely innocent of economic theory, left or right. It was in the interests of what he called "decency" that he set aside vast areas for national parks and forests, or tackled giant industries which, he believed, were not giving the public a square deal. Big Steel was outraged when, early in the Square Deal, the White House asked to see its books. "There's no stock ticker in the White House," J. P. Morgan was once told firmly by T.R.'s attorney general. Morgan was stricken by this unfeeling remark. With genuine naïveté, Teddy Roosevelt could not understand his growing unpopularity with the rich. He came home from a visit to Boston deeply hurt because only one man in the Harvard Club had been willing to speak to him. At the same time (just as J.F.K. was later involved in investigating labor rackets) Teddy Roosevelt stood up with equal firmness to labor unions when he thought they were wrong—as he not infrequently did.

T.R. could have told his successor a thing or two about Mississippi. Half a century ago, after Teddy Roosevelt asked a Mississippi Negro named Booker T. Washington to a meal at the White House, a vast and bitter uproar came from the South. No Southern lady, it was said, could enter the White House thereafter. When Mississippi hoodlums drove their Negro postmistress out of town, Teddy exercised Federal authority; he closed the post office.

It is of course pure coincidence that T.R. was repeatedly concerned, as President, with Cuba; it isn't so generally known that his administration, too, once came fairly near war with Russia, although over a very different matter. (The Czar rejected, unread, an angry protest from Washington against a pogrom.) There were warlike rumblings on occasion from Japan and Germany, too. T.R. believed, as his successor does, that there is serious danger in letting a foreign power underestimate American strength, and he believed in demonstrating our power. ("Speak softly, but carry a big stick.") He had neither Polaris submarines nor astronauts to send around the world, but he did have a Navy, and he used it. It was then generally thought impossible, because of coaling and other difficulties, for a battle fleet to circumnavigate the globe—and when this was proposed, New York and Philadelphia protested violently that they would certainly be shelled while the fleet was away. Nevertheless T.R. sent the Great White Fleet around the world; and its voyage proved, as we should say today, a successful deterrent.

Teddy Roosevelt's distinctive, rather high-pitched Harvard

voice was mimicked across the nation (although not on phonograph records) and so were his phrases (for "Vigah!" read "Bully for you!"). He had the knack of being quite a character, even a figure of fun, without losing stature as a national leader. Even before he was President, Times Square hawkers used to sell whistles in the shape of "Teddy Teeth." Children went to bed hugging Teddy bears—named for a real bear cub which T.R., on a hunting expedition, insisted should be set free. In the 1912 campaign he was amused by an opposition handbill which invited the public to Grant Park "to see Colonel Roosevelt walk on the waters of Lake Michigan." As he approached London, after his big-game hunting trip to Africa, *Punch* showed Trafalgar Square plastered with signs: "Do Not Shoot These Lions."

Teddy Roosevelt had, of course, his faults. (So has his successor, but no parallels will be attempted here.) Once, at least, in the matter of scarcely discouraging a revolution in Panama (it helped him obtain the land for the Canal), he was a bit of an international bully. At home, he could rave and rant. When his wife one day protested that he was urging the children to overexert themselves, he exclaimed loudly that he had rather see them die than grow up as "weaklings and cowards." (Young Quentin and Archie, who overheard, approached him at bedtime with a proposition. "Father, we have been talking it over and decided that if anyone must die, it should be the baby.")

He had been himself a very sickly boy—far more so than J.F.K.—and throughout his life he overcompensated, violently. It can be exhausting just to think about T.R. at play. He lost the sight of an eye in a White House boxing match, and once played ninety-one tennis games in a day. (Because of his eye trouble, he simply held up the ball to smash it in a serve. And of course he played right on through the rain.) He once killed a mountain lion while his companions held him upside down from a cliff. In his campaign of 1912 on the Progressive ticket ("we stand at Armageddon, and we battle for the Lord") he was shot—and spoke for an hour and a half with the bullet still in his body, for a cause which he had always known was hopeless. And afterward his idea of relaxation was an exploring trip in Brazil, where he almost died and from which he returned permanently weakened. "It was my last chance to be a boy," he explained. And thus he bore out a shrewd observation by his good friend, the British diplomat Spring-Rice: "You must always remember that the President is about six."

Clearly, this parlor game can only be carried so far. There are profound differences, as well as resemblances, between Theodore Roosevelt and John F. Kennedy. Today the big stick carried by the United States has a nuclear warhead, and no one, as a result, will ever call Mr. Kennedy "about six." He is not one to espouse a lost cause—much less risk his life needlessly in its behalf. His own competitiveness—and that of his whole romping, rollicking family—stems not from

childhood difficulties, but from the simple fact that they are Kennedys, the descendants of Irish immigrants who have made, and are still making, good. Not only a back injury, but a conventional and calculating temperament, make certain that he will not become "another Teddy Roosevelt."

And yet in some ways Mr. Kennedy, and all of us for that matter, have a lot to learn from Teddy Roosevelt. His antics have tended to submerge the memory of his ideas, but some of those ideas are surprisingly relevant today. For several decades, beginning perhaps with the Great Depression, the American concept of morality, of conscience, has become increasingly "social" and less and less personal. Teddy Roosevelt calls us back to the obvious truth, that morality is both personal *and* social—two sides of the same coin. His idea of democracy rested on a firm basis of individual decency and self-reliance and, when he was not lambasting the trusts and the "malefactors of great wealth," he preached this gospel constantly. ("The White House is a bully pulpit!" he exclaimed with enthusiasm.) What he said was hardly new, yet people listened to him: a man is not a good citizen if he does not behave well in his own family; he has to be a good breadwinner, a trusted neighbor; everyone's first duty is to carry his own weight. "Men can never escape being governed. Either they must govern themselves or they must submit to being governed by others."

Mr. Kennedy, too, has definite gifts as a preacher of the moral basis of democracy—as his inaugural address showed —and perhaps he could help us all to keep our balance in this dangerous, slippery time if he developed these gifts further. T.R.'s idea of morality—and this will surprise those who have thought of him only as a flag-waving nationalist— was international, too. He viewed World War I, for example, as essentially a conflict between right and wrong—an old-fashioned viewpoint of that struggle, which is now beginning to come back in style. He thought it indecent for Americans to get rich by selling munitions to the Allies who did our fighting for us. He pleaded, in vain, with President Wilson to be allowed to lead volunteer divisions to France, and took the refusal hard. It is possible to understand both his eagerness and the reluctance of the Wilson administration.

Even before the sinking of the *Lusitania* he had been advocating American intervention—and events seem to have proved him right, for an earlier end to World War I would not only have saved millions of lives in the trenches but quite possibly could have prevented the collapse of Russia, the rise of communism, and of Hitler, too. But these are speculations which ignore many political realities of that era.

Nor was he (in spite of some foolish talk about the nobility of war) essentially bellicose. Many years before, in accepting the Nobel Peace Prize for his part in settling the Russo-Japanese War, Theodore Roosevelt had been one of the first Americans to propose publicly the need for a league of nations to enforce the peace. He was ahead of Wilson here. And as the guns thundered in World War I, Teddy Roosevelt, now out of office, returned with—well, vigor—to this theme. He was explicit on the need for a world police force to enforce world law, and for nations to surrender their unlimited sovereignty. He recognized that it would be hard work to bring this about. But there was no sense in waiting until a band of angels descended to occupy the chancelleries of the world. The job would have to be done now, with the sort of nations now existing, just as it must be done today, by the brave and active man who has so often reminded us of Teddy Roosevelt. Should we not be willing to help in any possible way—even to take exercise, if necessary?

But, thank you, I think I'll sit out the touch football game.

Archie Robertson, a former information specialist for the U.S. Government, is an editor of The Lamp *magazine. He has written several books, including* That Old-Time Religion.

ALL ILLUSTRATIONS COURTESY OF SIR JOHN SOANE MUSEUM

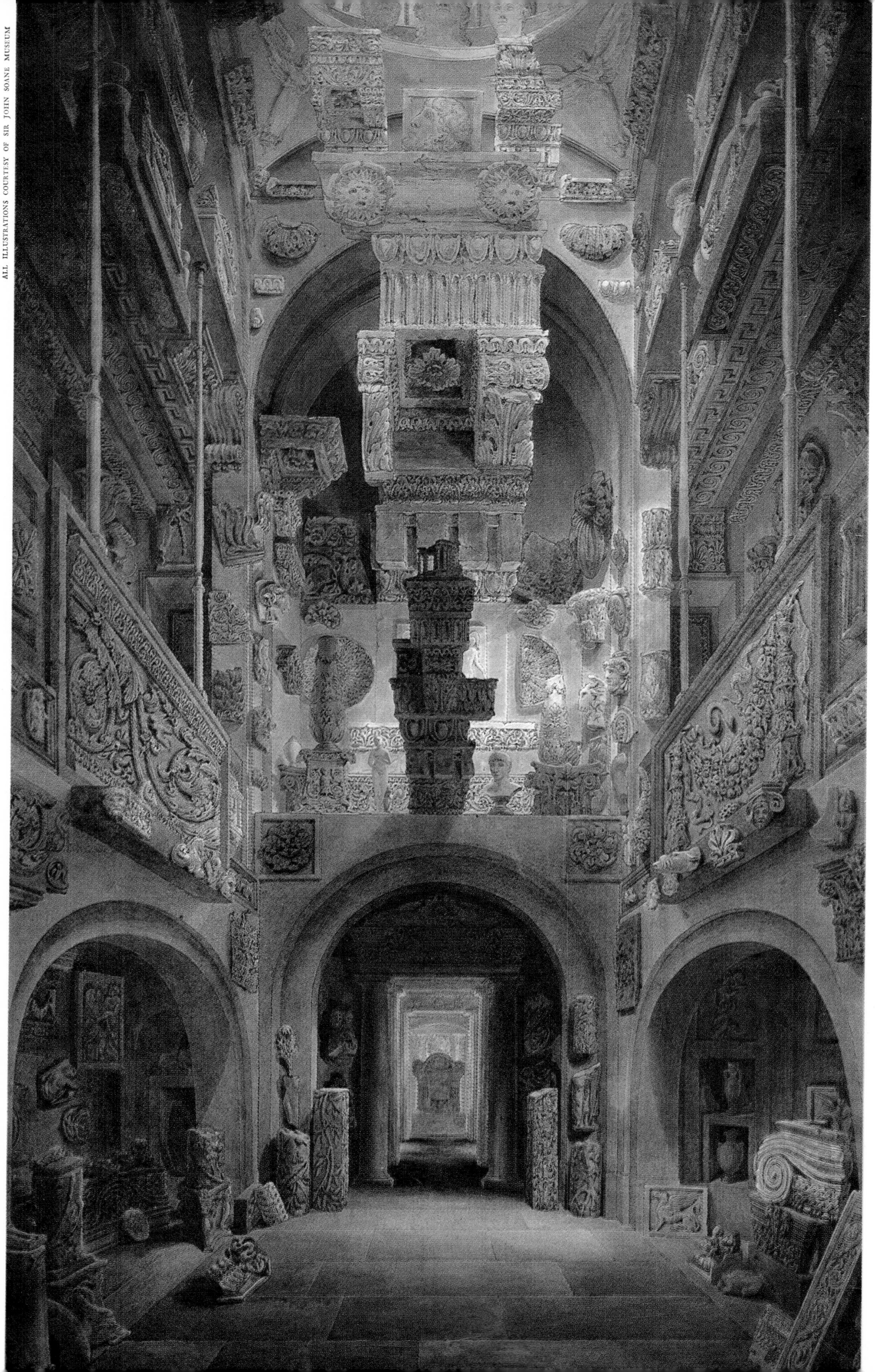

MAGPIE'S NEST
in a London Mansion

Karnak? Nineveh? Tyre?   No. A jam-packed city

house where Sir John Soane assembled a personal collection of odds

and ends in the early 1800's and taught young architects their trade

In my childhood I possessed a private "museum"—the name I gave to a small brightly painted wooden box, which contained a flint from an eighteenth-century flintlock gun, a number of old coins, a South American nut, a gold-and-green exotic beetle, odds and ends of Romano-British pottery, and some ancient clay tobacco pipes. Though at the time I did not suspect it, my collection had a long and distinguished ancestry and was formed on much the same principles as many famous collections of the past. Until a comparatively recent period, few museum curators attempted to arrange their exhibits according to a strictly scientific method.

Both Oxford's original Ashmolean, founded with the help of the celebrated antiquary Elias Ashmole in the year 1677, and the earlier Museum Tradescantianum, popularly called "Tradescant's Ark," were designed as, above all else, "Cabinets of Curiosities." John Tradescant and his son, for example, were naturalists and royal gardeners who, between them, examined the flora and fauna of Europe from Russia to the Balearic Islands. In 1637 the younger Tradescant visited the American Colonies, gathering wherever he went the precious botanical specimens with which he stocked his garden and his London house. Among the trees and shrubs they both introduced to England were the lilac, the acacia, and

the occidental plane tree. The descriptive catalogue the son presently published shows the diversity of both Tradescants' interests. Besides the herbs they grew in their "physic garden," it lists birds, quadrupeds, fish, shells, insects, mineral specimens, fruits, weapons, medals, and outlandish costumes.

Such were the curiosities that travelers flocked to see: unfamiliar and beautiful plants; the stuffed carcasses of strange beasts; gaudy shells arranged in pleasing patterns; fragments of metal and stone that recalled the genius of former ages; weapons that illustrated the manners and customs of remote, barbaric peoples—anything, in fact, that stirred the imagination and aroused a sense of awe and wonder. Compared with these early collections, the museum as it developed during the second half of the nineteenth century became a kind of scientifically arranged warehouse. True, modern curators, their eye on the general public, nowadays often adopt a more attractive mode of presentation. But there are still many scholars who feel that the museums over which they preside should be reserved, as far as possible, for the use of the learned specialist alone, and that the ordinary visitor is a tiresome intruder, to be tolerated but not unnecessarily encouraged.

Meanwhile the old "Cabinets of Curiosities" had been

In 1813 Soane's museum looked much as it does today: a compound of antique sculpture, plaster casts, eerie lighting, and horror vacui.

By PETER QUENNELL

closed and broken up. All except one. In 1813 the renowned architect Sir John Soane moved into the house he had built for himself overlooking a pleasant London square, and installed the heterogeneous collection that he had gradually been assembling. At No. 13, Lincoln's Inn Fields he established the museum that was to be his private monument. But before we consider the monument, we must turn our attention to the man. Sir John Soane's Museum is a remarkable edifice, and bears the imprint of a remarkable personality.

Its founder was born in September, 1753, the son of a modest country builder, and at the age of fifteen entered the office of George Dance the younger, whose grim masterpiece was Newgate Prison, where, above the windows, garlands of fetters took the place of the customary classical decorative wreaths. After two years, however, he joined Henry Holland, partner of "Capability" Brown, that well-known reformer of the English landscape who owed his nickname to the habit of assuring his employers that their ancestral pleasure grounds, he felt sure, were "capable of great improvement." Next Soane obtained a scholarship—"the most fortunate event in my life"—which made it possible to visit Italy; and there he secured a rich and highly eccentric

patron, Frederick Augustus Hervey, Bishop of Derry, who soon afterward added a coronet to his miter and entered the House of Lords as the fourth Earl of Bristol. "The Building Bishop" was devoted to architecture; and under his wing Soane studied the antiquities of Naples and the temples of Paestum, which left a lasting impression on his mind.

Soon after his return to England, Soane contracted a sensible and happy marriage. Elizabeth Smith, the niece of a prosperous builder, became his wife in 1784 and bore him two sons, John and George, neither of whom was destined to turn out well. By the middle of the decade Soane had already begun to make his way; and in 1788 he was appointed architect and surveyor to the Bank of England, a post he held for forty-five years. Then, in 1790, his wife's uncle died, bequeathing Soane a comfortable fortune. He was now free of economic anxieties and could settle down to develop his own style, which until his death he continued to impose upon a lengthy series of private and official buildings.

Soane's style has been described as "Romantic-Classicism"; and although some English writers are inclined to regard his work as merely "a quaint cul-de-sac . . . off the

Portrait of Soane, 1830, by Sir Thomas Lawrence

main line of English architectural development," foreign
critics, we are told, recognize him as "one of the greatest
English figures in the general late eighteenth- and early
nineteenth-century artistic movement." His predecessors had
been predominantly English, but Soane learned much from
Continental theorists—for instance, from the Abbé Pierre
Laugier, of whose revolutionary treatise, *Essai sur l'architecture,* he acquired as many as eleven copies. But his method
was eclectic, and Gothic and Renaissance motifs were often
woven into a classical design. Since his childhood, he wrote,
he had been in love with architecture, and throughout his
whole life he "pursued it with the intensity of a passion."
What he sought was "the poetry of the architecture," and
he attempted to achieve it not only through the proportions
and details of an edifice but through dramatic and ingenious
effects of lighting. A beautiful structure was to be the realiza-
tion of a dream, stately and dignified but also somehow
strange; and when his friend J. M. Gandy produced a pan-
oramic drawing of Soane's assembled church designs (pages
78–79), he littered the foreground with fragments of antique
temples that would have appealed to Poussin or Claude Lor-
rain, and gave it a background of wild and bosky hills.

Despite his prosperity, Soane was an indefatigable worker,
perpetually traveling, sometimes in his carriage, sometimes
on foot, and spending seven or eight hours at his drawing
board, every day of the week except Sunday. John and
George disappointed him; and George is said to have broken
his mother's heart by publishing an unfavorable reference
to his father's talents. During Soane's last period of creative
activity, from 1820 to his death in 1837, the "dear old ty-
rant"—his enthusiasm wore out the youths he employed—
became increasingly remote and odd. Very tall and thin, he
was dressed, wrote one of these assistants, "entirely in black;
his waistcoat being of velvet, and he wore knee-breeches
with silk stockings . . . it can be scarcely said that he had
any front face. In profile his countenance was extensive; but
looking at it 'edgeways' it would have been 'to any thick
sight' something of the invisible. A brown wig carried the
elevation of his head to the almost unattainable height; so
that his physiognomy was suggestive of the picture which is
presented on the back of a spoon held vertically."

Thus he appears in Sir Thomas Lawrence's portrait; we
imagine him, sitting at the fireside, shielding his red-rimmed
eyes against the blaze, while the same assistant, George

Wightwick, read aloud from *Gil Blas*. "P-o-o-r Gil! p-o-o-r Gil!" Soane would murmur reflectively. Bereaved of his wife, who had died in 1815, saddened by the behavior of his sons (both of whom made unfortunate marriages), troubled with turbulent romantic visions he could never quite translate into stone and brick, he himself was not a happy man. Yet he had consolations—none more soothing perhaps than the museum he had built up around him, and which, after his death, according to a special Act of Parliament inscribed five years earlier, he bequeathed to his countrymen "for the benefit of the public." He was eighty-three when he died, leaving behind a meticulous *Description* of the house in which he had spent nearly a quarter of a century.

Primarily, it is a monument to the owner's taste. Soane had built the house, and also furnished it, down to such minor domestic features as the grates and fire irons; the collection it encloses was carefully arranged to reflect his general frame of mind. At first sight it is a gigantic magpie's nest. But as Henry-Russell Hitchcock remarks, there is something "almost Surrealist" about "the organized clutter of disparate objects" in the domed crypt. Gandy's rather fanciful water color (page 72), even more vividly than the existing arrangement, suggests the effect that Soane intended to achieve. Ledge after ledge lines the walls of a narrow, lofty, shaftlike chamber running up through the house from the basement to the topmost floor; and walls and ledges and innumerable brackets are laden with broken masses of antique sculpture, bits of capital and frieze and plinth, Roman statuettes and portrait heads, lion masks and occasional tombs and vases, all bathed in a dim, mysterious glow.

This atmosphere of mystery the architect did his best to evoke even in the more modern rooms. He liked to produce an effect of depth and, whenever he could, contrived a vista; so that although No. 13, Lincoln's Inn Fields is not a very large house, it resembles a romantic labyrinth, offering endless surprises and strange discoveries as the visitor slowly threads its maze. Here is a Gothic fantasy named the "Monk's Parlor," and through its window we glimpse the

medieval cloister that Soane constructed from scraps of fifteenth-century stonework he appropriated while restoring the old Palace of Westminster. The "Catacombs" are full of funerary urns; the "Sepulchral Chamber" enshrines the sarcophagus of Seti I, removed from the Valley of the Kings in 1817.

There are a "Flaxman Recess" and a "Shakespeare Niche." The "Picture Room," added in 1824, contains two of Hogarth's finest pictorial series: *The Election,* which is among his noblest achievements, and his earlier representations of the Rake's tragedy. Hogarth and Watteau rub shoulders with Reynolds and Turner, Greco-Roman marbles with contemporary plaster casts; places are found for illuminated manuscripts, a silver watch reputed to have belonged to Sir Christopher Wren, and a jewel said to have been discovered in Charles I's baggage after the Battle of Naseby.

Few men have compressed so much of themselves into so limited a private setting. Monuments are defaced, houses are pulled down. Every year twentieth-century London discards something of its individual quality as impersonal cosmopolitan buildings break the outlines of old-fashioned streets and squares. But if Sir John Soane were suddenly to re-emerge beneath the plane trees of Lincoln's Inn Fields and cross the threshold of his old house, he would notice very little change. Seti's sarcophagus has lost its blue lining, and its alabaster is now somewhat darkened; the plaster casts are a trifle yellower; the mirrors Soane so cleverly installed to add a new perspective to the breakfast room are growing silvery and dim with age. Otherwise his monument is unspoiled, and likely to remain unspoiled so long as Acts of Parliament are honored. The average museum pays its tribute to the genius of humanity at large. The value of Sir John Soane's Museum does not depend either on the breadth of its scope or on the value of its contents. It is a record of the lifelong adventures of a single adventurer's imagination.

Peter Quennell, whose appreciation for the eighteenth century has engaged his interest in such colorful figures as William Hogarth and Fanny Hill, is coeditor of History Today.

Soane's successes as an architect began with his sketch for a triumphal bridge, left, which in 1778 won him a Gold Medal from the Royal Academy, an introduction to George III, and a grant to study in Rome. A complex pile of rotundas, arcades, and porticoes, this design only remotely resembles a bridge, but it does contain the essentials of Soane's mature neo-classic style. It also foretells the fondness for opulence and clutter that would find such exuberant expression in his museum, opposite. This apotheosis of all attics is "The Dome," a gallery devoted to such diverse attractions as Greek and Roman shards, a vase commemorating the Battle of Trafalgar, and contemporary works including a bust of Sir John himself.

In 1818, when Soane was at the peak of his official career, he was selected as one of three architects to lead a low-cost church-building program for London's expanding suburbs. This drawing, lovingly rendered by Soane's most notable pupil, J. M. Gandy, provided government commissioners with a picturesque catalogue of his master's designs, all based on the floor plan in the foreground. Fortunately for Soane's modern reputation, economy intervened where taste failed, and the borrowed splendors of Tudor, Norman, Gothic, and Potluck lost out to a more congenial neo-classic idiom in the three churches he eventually executed.

Turnerelli's George III
in Roman habit

Cast of Pallas Athene,
possibly model for early
19th-century Britannia coins

Ephesian Diana,
a Roman copy

Roman torso,
black marble

Copy of a *torchère*
from the Villa Borghese

Tomb of Seti I, 1300 B.C.

Roman cinerary urn

From an Egyptian sarcophagus to a pair of dried cats, nothing was refused the unexclusive society of Soane's burgeoning collection, shown in this profi

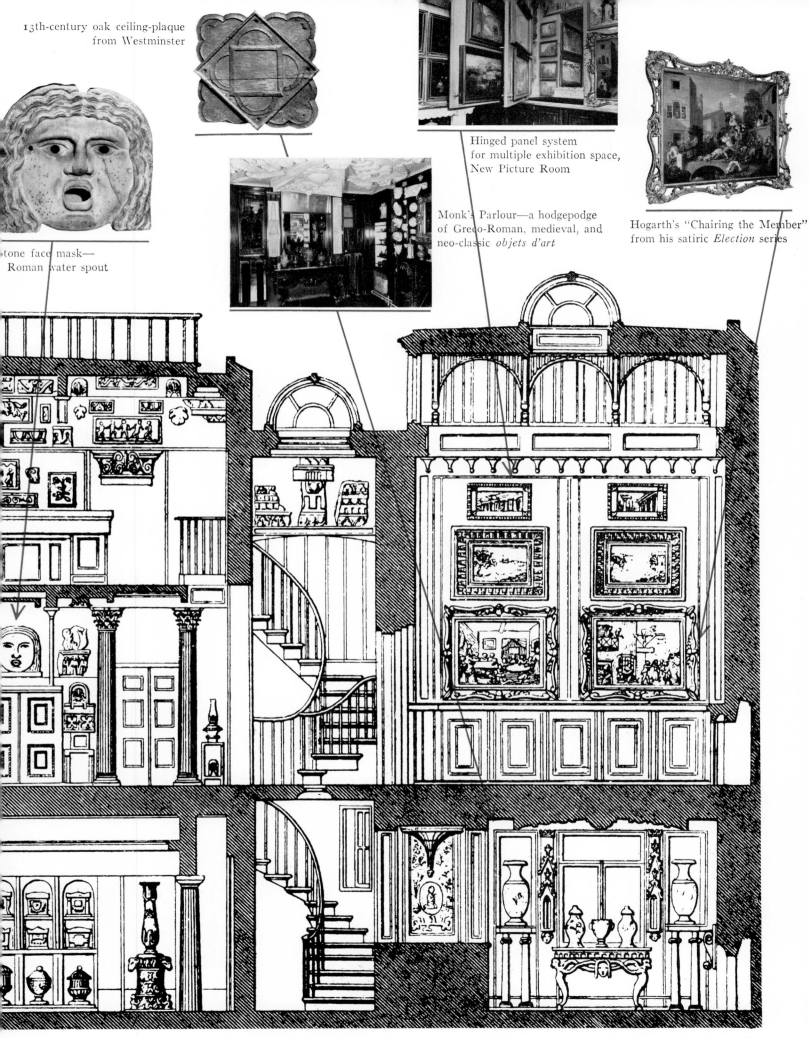

13th-century oak ceiling-plaque
from Westminster

Hinged panel system
for multiple exhibition space,
New Picture Room

Monk's Parlour—a hodgepodge
of Greco-Roman, medieval, and
neo-classic *objets d'art*

Hogarth's "Chairing the Member"
from his satiric *Election* series

...tone face mask—
...Roman water spout

...e galleries as they were arranged in 1827. Thanks to the loyalty of its custodians, the museum is still a monument to one man's search for immortality

Soane's chief work—the piecemeal reconstruction of the Bank of England—remains his most splendid achievement. Beginning in 1795, he designed a screen wall to encircle the huge complex, with the colonnaded corner inspired by the Temple at Tivoli, top, its most imposing feature. Within the bank, demands for improved fireproof construction and skylighting spurred him to throw off such classical loyalties. In the Old Dividend, or 4%, Office, above, the solution was a soaring domed vault remarkable for its structural clarity and restraint.

The Court of Chancery (below) was one of seven courts included in a building Soane designed within the old grounds of the Palace of Westminster. Though the architect had set out to erect a neo-classic structure, public passions forced him to tear down the partially built shell and replace it with a Gothic façade. When completed in 1825, the courts revealed a common rectangular plan and various adaptations of Soane's highly individual skylit ceilings. Such details as the hanging arches over the gallery and the elaborately carved brackets above it must have further mollified a younger generation that was moving vigorously toward the Gothic revival.

Side-Street Painter, or

Shopping with

There is a story, probably apocryphal, about a novelist who started writing because he wanted to learn to type. There is another story, probably true, about an artist named Sivard, who started to paint because his wife wanted a souvenir picture of Paris.

Robert Sivard was born in New York in 1914, studied art at Pratt Institute, the National Academy of Design, the Académie Julien in Paris, and worked for some years as a commercial artist and art director. In 1949 he moved to Paris with a job as director of visual information for the United States Embassy. After Sunday-painting his first "souvenir," a French grocery store, Sivard found he couldn't stop, and his government job has given him a chance to paint shop fronts in Moscow, Havana, San Juan, Rome, New York, and in Washington, D.C., where he now lives with his wife and two children.

Sivard is an anachronism today—a painter who is interested in subject matter more than technique. He packs a canvas full of bits of graffiti to decipher, tattered plaster, and hand-lettered signs to peer at; his subject is that hardy breed, the small businessman, the shopkeeper. And he faces these shops and shopkeepers from close-up, head-on; from a perspective that implies the eye level of a serious, but not somber, adult. These are portraits, as Sivard says, "not of the individual alone but of the urban scene. The portraitist searches for the character-revealing details, the wear and tear of life. He must be close enough to see texture and character flaws, the creases of age and the lines of laughter. Old cities, like Paris and Rome, have had time to develop laugh wrinkles. . . . The character lines of a city, and its civilization, are in its side streets. *Les petites rues* are the heart of Paris. Remove them and the soul of the city will be gone even though the Seine still flows and great monuments remain."

Sivard has not set himself a monumental task, to be sure; but it is work done out of joy rather than anguish and, as such, has found a universally warm reception. The original inspiration for most of the pictures in these pages came from particular establishments that caught Sivard's fancy, but the final painting is usually a composite of details gleaned from a number of shops. In combining the various elements Sivard feels he pretty much does "what the proprietor wished he could afford to do." Happily, Sivard does not expect to run out of small businesses to paint. As he said when he found a thriving group of streetwalkers in Russia, "I was happy to see that the sisterhood has an active chapter in Moscow. Free enterprise shall not die."

Robert Sivard and Mme Celesta, the fortuneteller opposite, have much in common. Both read character lines—Sivard those of the city, Mme Celesta those of a man's hand—and although Sivard is no prophet, he and the lady both delight in showing us tidbits of our past and present, represented in crystal balls, cartes et tarots, and horoscopes. Mme Celesta is not based on any one person but is the artist's conception of the archetypal tea-leaf reader whose colorful caravan is her home as well as her place of business. Cats and domesticity go together in Sivard's paintings like Paris and Pernod.

Sivard took considerable comic license with the Paris shops on this page, even claiming ownership of the two at right. Dealers in horseflesh (recognizable by the horse-head emblems) are not uncommon in Paris, though the banner announcing a "Special on Mule" does seem bizarre. The shoemaker's shop, at far right, contains a flash of wit in the unobtrusive sign: "Man with right leg seeks man with left leg. Object: exchange shoes." Professor Tramond, below, is blessed with two cats to make his shop homey—one sits at his feet, while he holds the other affectionately in his hand.

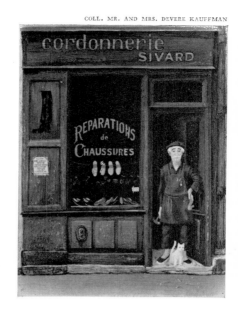

Les petites rues.

When a Parisian describes extreme old age he says "vieux comme les rues," not "old as the hills." Translating that idea to his canvases, Sivard avoids transient passers-by and plants immobile proprietors in front of these three cafés. A La Locomotive is a composite of typical spots, and Au Rendez-vous des Pecheurs is a redesigned Seine café, enhanced by the presence of the girl standing under the sign "Furnished Rooms." Au Nègre Joyeux, now a grocery store, existed in the 1920's as Sivard has drawn it here; it was a Left Bank artist's hangout and an old haunt of Hemingway's.

he anatomy of Paris

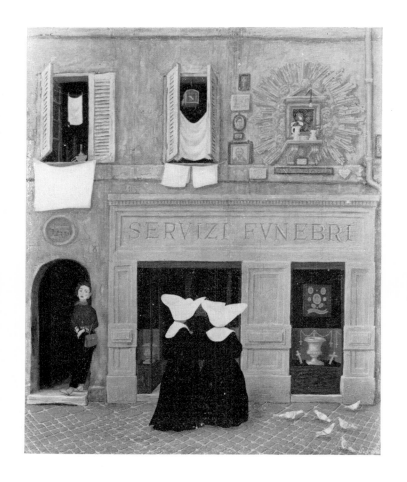

MIDTOWN GALLERIES, N.Y.

Side-street beat from Rome to New York

The streetwalker, according to Sivard, belongs to "an international sisterhood which has a standard issue of large patent-leather handbags." To prove his point Sivard has painted a girl in Havana, at left, near a jewelry store; in Rome, above left, with a contingent from a different international sisterhood, in front of a shop selling articles for decorating graves; and in Moscow, above right, in a painting titled Private Trader.

Pepe's Live Poultry Market, opposite, is in the kosher warehouse district around East 105th Street in New York. Sivard recalled the market from his youth and, for the final version of the painting, combined it with an old firehouse he had seen elsewhere. That Pepe sells gallinas vivas *(live hens) is attested by the trash cans overflowing with freshly plucked feathers.*

Peripheral vision

Most of Sivard's paintings seem to say that the small detail one sees out of the corner of the eye offers frequently the most delightful, and meaningful, glimpse of life. Sometimes, as in the paintings shown here, a fleeting observation becomes the center of attention. At left above, Sivard has placed on the steps of a Paris Métro station a nun, whose pleated wimple forms a contrapuntal visual joke with the art nouveau *canopy halo over her. The hammer and sickle in the Russian bakery, above right, inspire the children not so much with thoughts of the Revolution as with longing for the cookies, sugar pretzels, and other sweets that hold these emblems aloft. Opposite, Sivard has placed Ambassador George V. Allen, former head of the United States Information Agency, in a newsstand displaying the enormous variety of* USIA *publications. Sivard worked for the Ambassador starting in 1958 and continued in his post as director of exhibits for the Agency after Allen left in 1960. Sivard now has a studio on the top floor of his home, where he retreats three or four nights a week for several hours of painting. What continues to distinguish his work, and to delight his admirers, is an eye that captures at a glance the momentarily disappearing detail and sees in that seemingly insignificant encounter something of a joke, a truth, and a sense of permanence.*

These two panels, executed almost two hundred years after the event by Miguel Gonzales, show Cortes riding into Mexico City
—unaware that he is playing the role of a supernatural being—and the emperor Montezuma being carried out to welcome him.

THE DAY THE GOD CAME BACK

By J. H. ELLIOTT

or ten years Montezuma II, Emperor of the Aztecs, had been troubled by news of strange portents. Comets traversed the skies for hours at a time; the waters of Lake Texcoco foamed and boiled and flooded the capital; the temple of the god of war mysteriously caught fire; and disembodied voices filled the air with groans and lamentations. Worst of all, a bird like a crane, with a mirror on the crown of its head, was captured and brought to Montezuma; and when he looked into the mirror, he saw an ill-omened constellation of stars which suddenly changed into a scene of armed men mounted on deer.

Anxiously, Montezuma summoned his priests and astrologers, and put them to death when they failed to answer his questions. He ordered more slaves to be sacrificed, in the hope of averting disaster. But in his heart he knew—indeed he was soon expressly informed by a talking stone—that it was already too late. For the omens could only presage the imminent return of Quetzalcoatl, the Plumed Serpent, the god-king of "a grave countenance, white-skinned and bearded," who had long ago been driven from his Mexican kingdom, and would one day come back, traveling from the east, to recover his lost inheritance.

How are we to interpret the deep anguish of Montezuma at the prospect of the second coming of Quetzalcoatl? At least the portents could be no cause for surprise, for it had long been known that the Plumed Serpent would one day return to assume what was rightfully his. Montezuma's Aztecs had inherited this tradition from the Toltecs, who had inhabited ancient Mexico. Montezuma himself, although the leader of a warrior people, was by temperament a philosopher-king, deeply attracted by Toltec beliefs. During long hours of meditation in his house of retreat he seems to have developed doubts and uncertainties concerning the contradictions between these older beliefs and the primitive religion of the Aztecs, into which they had never been fully absorbed. He was profoundly uneasy about the mood in which Quetzalcoatl would return to his kingdom; he felt a sense of responsibility to his people, and at the same time a personal guilt that Quetzalcoatl should choose his reign in which to return; and he had premonitions, now confirmed by the portents, that it was his fate to preside over the destruction of Aztec civilization.

The doubts that tormented Montezuma perhaps symbolized, in a heightened and personal form, a mental conflict in the society over which he presided as a semi-divine king. To all outward appearances the Aztec state was strong and prosperous. Since founding Tenochtitlan (Mexico City) in 1325, the Aztecs had conquered the neighboring tribes of Central America, and helped preserve their domination by an elaborate system of religious terror, whereby the Aztec priests made it understood that the wrath of the implacable deities who ruled the universe could be averted only by a constant orgy of human sacrifice. But the heavy apparatus of ecclesiastical despotism, decked with all the trappings of blood-stained ceremonial, had not prevented the evolution among the Aztecs of a vigorous and dynamic society. By the time of Montezuma II this society had emerged from its primitive tribal pattern into a complex state-structure, with a privileged ruling class and a prosperous mercantile community; and the city of Tenochtitlan, with more than 300,000 inhabitants, had become the powerful and wealthy head of the confederation of cities which together constituted the Aztec empire. It is not surprising that these rapid material developments were

Haccompanied by some signs of spiritual stress, and that, well before the reign of Montezuma, the necessity for the endless shedding of human blood had come to be questioned. Thus it may be that the insistent reports of the imminent return of Quetzalcoatl served to confirm doubts that Montezuma shared with some of his subjects— doubts about the system of which he was the supreme head, and whether that system would meet with the approval of Quetzalcoatl, a god who traditionally was opposed to the sacrifice of human victims.

ow, then, should Montezuma prepare for the coming of Quetzalcoatl? Should he do penance, or flee, or put an end to his life? But then what would become of his people? And could he indeed be absolutely certain that Quetzalcoatl would, after all, return? But on this score at least, doubt was soon to be silenced. During the first third of the doom-laden year One Reed, or more precisely on March 12, 1519, the fleet of Hernando Cortes anchored off Tabasco. The Spaniards had come to Mexico.

Hastily, the watchers whom Montezuma had posted all along the coasts of his dominions sent their long-awaited news to the Emperor. At the very moment when the white god Quetzalcoatl was most expected from out of the east, he had in fact appeared. At last the terrible years of uncertainty were over. This of itself was momentarily sufficient to revive Montezuma's spirits: now he could do something; he could act, instead of merely wait. He promptly dispatched messengers to greet Quetzalcoatl-Cortes, bearing with them costly jewels and ornaments, including some that belonged to Quetzalcoatl himself and had been kept in readiness against his eventual return. But when the messengers brought back their tales of the white-faced visitors, and described the strange animals on which they rode, and the thunder of their guns, "Montezuma feared very much, and was greatly dismayed." Again he made sacrifices and consulted his priests, but this time he decided to send out enchanters to deflect the unwelcome visitors from their path; he might still deter them, either by sorcery or with valuable gifts, from setting foot in Tenochtitlan. But the sorcery availed nothing, and the gifts merely strengthened the resolution of Cortes and his men to arrive at the court of so opulent a prince. As they came closer and closer to the capital, joined on their march by warriors from subject races who had seized the occasion to revolt against the oppressive Aztec regime, the unhappy Montezuma lost heart. "He wanted to escape; he wanted to flee. . . . He wanted to hide himself from the gods. And he could not hide. . . . And so he resolved to await his enemies, to be brave . . . to finish with his doubts, and to resign himself to what should afterwards come."

It was on November 8, 1519, that Cortes and his band of less than four hundred Spaniards rode down the great causeway across Lake Texcoco into the city of Tenochtitlan. This was the moment they had been waiting for since August, when they had turned their backs on the coast and marched resolutely into the interior of an unknown land, forcing their way through narrow ravines, crossing vast tracts of desert beneath a burning sun, toiling up steep mountain passes in the icy cold. Already those long months of hardship and privation seemed to belong to legend, for as one of the company would someday write, "What men have there been in the world who have known such daring?" But to them nothing was more extraordinary in this whole extraordinary expedition than the reception they had been given along the route. The Indians had risen to greet them, and the great warrior Montezuma had sent, not troops, but gifts. Now they were on the brink of their goal, within sight of the wondrous city which appeared to them in the distance like "the enchantments they tell of in the legend of Amadis, on account of the great towers and temples and buildings rising from the water"; and, most astonishing of all, the city stood open to receive them. Was Montezuma, then, leading them into a carefully baited trap? As they slowly progressed down the causeway, pressing through the great crowds that had turned out to stare,

In this sketch by an Aztec artist Cortes and his prisoner Montezuma confer peacefully, with the help of Cortes's interpreter Doña Marina.

Cortes and his men instinctively remembered the warnings they had been given, that "we should beware of entering Mexico, where they would kill us, as soon as they had us inside." And they held their weapons tight.

But this was no trap. Cortes, knowing nothing of the divine role in which Montezuma had cast him, was alert to any hint of treachery. Yet at the same time he had an invincible faith in "the Creator and Mover of all things"—in a God whose chosen instrument he was, and who had preserved him for His special purposes. The Providence that had watched over him so far would not desert him now. Entirely unable to comprehend why the Aztecs should receive him in this fashion, but convinced that it was part of God's inscrutable design, he therefore went forward in the certainty that somehow all would be well. On past the bridge he went, and found two long processions of Aztec lords advancing to greet him; behind them came Montezuma himself, borne on a litter under a canopy, "richly attired according to his usage . . . shod with sandals, the soles . . . of gold and the upper part adorned with precious stones." The litter stopped and Montezuma descended, stepping onto cloths that had been laid to prevent his feet from touching the earth. Supported by two kinsmen, he advanced toward Cortes, while the nobles averted their eyes in reverence.

Two men, and two worlds, stood face to face. On one side stood an adventurer from the Spain of Charles V: the son of a poor hidalgo family from Extremadura; now thirty-four years old, a man "of a good height, well proportioned and of strong limbs, and the color of his face was rather ashy, and he was not very cheerful-looking. . . . His beard was dark and sparse and short . . . and his chest was high, and his back of a good shape, and he was lean . . . and somewhat bowlegged"; brave, astute, a born leader of men; a figure who represented in heightened form all the contrasting qualities of Renaissance Spain—at once curious and matter-of-fact, skeptical and deeply devout, convinced that nothing was impossible to man (or at least to Castilians), and yet that nothing could be achieved except through the will of God. Now, with that sense of absolute mastery which he always contrived to convey, he waited to greet the ruler of a vast and wealthy empire of which Europe had never even heard, knowing that, if he acted his part as became him, this empire might one day belong to Spain. Facing him was Montezuma II, supremely dignified at what was for him, as for Cortes, the greatest moment of his life. Montezuma looked no more than forty, although in fact he was fifty-two; "of good height and well proportioned, slender and spare of flesh, not very swarthy, but of the natural color and shade of an Indian. He did not wear his hair long, but so as just to cover his ears; his scanty beard was well shaped and thin." There was about Montezuma a natural majesty, as befitted the absolute ruler of ten million subjects; and although his customary self-command had in recent years been undermined by superhuman happenings in the cosmic drama in which he found himself involved, his doubts were nearly all dispelled as he prepared himself with becoming reverence to greet the returning god.

Cortes stepped forward to embrace him. "Is it perhaps you? Are you perhaps Montezuma?" But the Emperor of the Aztecs, caught up in the stiff ceremonial of his own formal world, was too sacred a figure to be touched, and the lords kept Cortes back. "Yes, it is I," replied Montezuma, inclining before him, and set himself to deliver his carefully rehearsed oration, translated by Cortes's Indian interpreter, Doña Marina, into something Cortes could understand—and yet not understand at all. "O Lord of ours, be welcome; with great trouble have you come here, to our house, to sit on your throne and your chair. . . . This indeed is what has been told us by the kings our predecessors, that you would come to see your city, and would sit on your throne, and your chair. Now what they said to us has come true. . . . Be welcome to this land; rest now; our lord has returned." And Cortes, in his usual precise manner tempered with effortless Castilian superiority, replied through Doña Marina: "Tell Montezuma to be of good cheer and fear nothing, for I love him well and so do all those who come with me. . . . We have been very happy to see him and know him—something we have wished to do for many a day, and our wish has been fulfilled. We have come to his house, Mexico; we shall see him and speak to him at leisure." Then Cortes removed the collar of pearls and glass beads he was wearing and put it round Montezuma's neck; and, shortly afterward, Montezuma's servants brought two necklaces made of red shells, from each of which hung "eight golden shrimps," and Montezuma placed them round Cortes's neck. These necklaces were insignia of Quetzalcoatl. The white god had come back to his own.

Much was to happen in the days that followed this extraordinary meeting, but the meeting itself had fixed a pattern from which there could be no escape. Both Cortes and Montezuma would play out the roles in which they had appeared on November 8, 1519—Cortes vigorous, decisive, always in command, skillfully preserving the initiative that he had so surprisingly acquired; Montezuma serene, now that he had performed his duties and welcomed Quetzalcoatl to his kingdom, and acquiescing in all that Cortes asked. On November 14 Cortes displayed once again his capacity for the supreme gamble—a capacity that would have been utterly reckless had it not been based on absolute certainty that the hand of Providence was with him—and took Montezuma prisoner in his own capital. During the months of Montezuma's captivity in Cortes's own house the two men saw much of each other, spending their mornings together in conversation or in playing the Mexican game of *totoloque*, in which golden disks were thrown onto golden pins. In the course of their conversations Cortes tried to tell Montezuma about the god of the Christians, but for all Montezuma's interest in foreign religions, Cortes's arguments made no impression. Their two worlds were too far apart for any meeting of minds. But, in a curious way, the gulf between captive and captors came to be spanned—not, as the Spaniards hoped, by religious conversion, but by the development of an instinctive mutual respect. The "great" Montezuma was never greater than in the days of his captivity, and the calm nobility of his character made a deep impression on Spaniards who found in their prisoner those very qualities which their own European code of chivalry had taught them to admire. When the Aztecs finally turned on the ruler whose inaction had betrayed them, and he was killed by a stone thrown by one of his own subjects, "Cortes wept for him, and all of us captains and soldiers, and there was no man among us who knew him and was intimate with him, who did not bemoan him as though he were our father, and it is not to be wondered at, considering how good he was."

Recoiling in horror from the blood-drenched world of the Aztecs, the Spanish conquerors were yet able to grieve for the ruler who had sacrificed thousands of victims. But if they admired the man, they had nothing but loathing for the system he represented. They would smash and destroy it, as Cortes had gone out one morning and smashed the idols in the great temple with an iron bar. In the end the Spaniards destroyed everything: the gods, the state, the civilization. Four hundred men conquered Mexico, but in reality the conquest had been half achieved before they set foot on its soil. For when the first omens were seen, before Cortes had ever heard speak of Mexico, Montezuma had already made his decision. In his person the world of the Aztecs resigned itself in the prime of life to the necessity of death; and, with the measured ceremonial ever attendant upon the worship of its pitiless gods, proceeded to offer itself up, under its emperor's direction, for the inevitable act of self-sacrifice.

J. H. Elliott is the author of The Revolt of the Catalans *and* Imperial Spain, *both published this year. He is a fellow of Trinity College at Cambridge, where he lectures in history, but is now on leave to study in the United States and in Mexico.*

HOW TO BUY A TUBA: NOT A SOUSAPHONE, NOT A FRENCH HORN, NOT A BARITONE, BUT A TUBA—A USED

UPRIGHT,

SHORT, FAT,

DOUBLE

B-FLAT

TUBA

(the kind you hold in your lap)

By JAMES J. FARAN, JR.

I have wanted to own a tuba for a long time. Let's not attempt a Freudian analysis of why I like the tuba; let's just say I like low notes, and the way music sounds when a tuba is putting a firm foundation under it. I'm one of the dwindling number of people left on earth who prefer the tuba to the string bass. From ancient Ted Weems dance recordings to the modern-day Dixieland of Turk Murphy, to *The Great Gate at Kiev*, I am enamored of the sound of the tuba.

My musical education began with the French horn in grade school, and I learned to play the sousaphone in high school and also played it in college. (The sousaphone is the large bass horn worn over the shoulder and played in marching bands; its bell appears above the head of its player, pointing forward directly down the street.) This, however, was not the kind of bass horn for which I yearned; the sousaphone is too large, too cold, and has too harsh a tone for indoor use. I wanted a short, fat, upright, double B-flat tuba of the kind you hold in your lap—the sort of horn whose gigantic bell appears majestically in the back row of a symphony orchestra during the playing of Wagner or Berlioz. Throughout my school and college years my mother often urged me to get a tuba, suggesting that I might pay for it by playing it. Unfortunately, we never had enough capital for the initial investment, even though tubas were considerably less expensive in those days.

In recent years, having launched four children into the world, and successfully (with my wife's help) gotten them through the diaper stage, I returned to my hobby of music. Opportunities to play came to me, first in a concert band (which does march on special occasions), and then in a Dixieland jazz band. As a starter, I bought myself a used baritone horn to play in the concert band. This instrument has a mouthpiece well suited to the embouchure of an out-of-practice amateur musician, and it is a lot of fun to play because it is so often given the countermelody (the trio of the march "Barnum and Bailey's Favorite," if you can recall it, has one of the most beautiful baritone countermelodies). The baritone soon proved inadequate for the Dixieland band, however, partly because it lacked the power to make itself heard, and partly because it is impossible to play on a valve instrument the trombone glissandi that are a trademark of Dixieland jazz.

My next acquisition was therefore a shiny new trombone, which I bought one Saturday afternoon and played the following Sunday night with the jazz band, although I had never played one before. While struggling to become proficient on the trombone, I switched back occasionally to the baritone and played tubalike parts on it. After all, the baritone looks like a miniature tuba, and plays just one octave higher; you might call it the poor man's tuba. Doing this stirred up the old desire for a tuba, and I began mentioning it in conversation and got a few leads, like word of someone's cousin who was about to get married and would therefore probably want to sell his tuba. In most cases the tuba turned out not to be a tuba after all, or it wasn't for sale, or it had already been sold.

Business takes me to New York City infrequently, but when I did get there, I took to walking past the music stores to see what I could see. The stores were always closed, as business kept me from prowling during normal working hours. One evening I saw four obviously used tubas in a store window, at least two of which looked interesting. When business again took me to New York, I made sure there was free time to go inquire about those old tubas. They were still there but the salesman told me bluntly, "You don't want any of them. Two are C-tubas, one is an E-flat, and the other is an F." He was right. Each of those horns was pitched higher than the B-flat, limiting the lower range of the instrument, and what is more important, the fingering was different from that of the B-flat horns, which is what I know. Every music dealer I talked to had no used B-flat tubas, and said he hadn't seen any in years.

Back home I heard about another used tuba for sale, and got excited when I was told the asking price: $125. But when I saw the instrument I lost interest immediately. It was an old Italian horn with rotary valve mechanisms, and the piping was arranged in Italian or middle-European style, which is difficult to describe except to say that the small piping, instead of being stiffly parallel, is bent into free-flowing, pear-shaped forms which I do not like. After having traveled all the way across town to see it, I didn't even pick it up to blow it.

My taste in tubas was definitely crystallizing. There was another feature of tuba appearance I was fussy about; I did not want one of the very tall, thin German tubas which are sometimes seen in symphonies. What I wanted was a short, fat tuba having the characteristics of American manufacture.

The well was apparently running dry on used tubas, so I wrote to a number of musical-instrument manufacturers asking for catalogues, specifications, and prices. Two companies replied that they had discontinued production of tubas (one had the gall to offer me a fiberglass sousaphone instead). Four sent catalogues which provided me with the first detailed information on new tubas I had ever seen. I went through the exquisite agony of trying to decide whether I wanted a bell-forward or an upright. (The bells of some tubas are bent forward à la sousaphone so as to project the sound more directly toward the audience. This is nice but it costs extra.) I also suffered from the "four-valve syndrome" for a while; again at extra cost, some tubas can be equipped with an additional valve which allows them to play lower by the musical interval of a fourth. I was cured of this disease by a musician friend acquainted with psychological disorders of this type, who convinced me that the added low range was completely useless in jazz and of only occasional value in orchestra work for producing slow, organ-like, pedal tones. In those four catalogues there was only one tuba I really liked the looks of, but, on checking with the local distributor, I found the manufacturer had failed to point out that he'd discontinued making tubas.

My perusal of the catalogues also revealed the financial drain involved in buying a new tuba. The list prices range from $900 to $1,250, and even with the discount it is possible to obtain from most dealers, this is a lot of money. I had to turn back to the seemingly hopeless search for a used one.

At length a friend told me there was an old tuba in with the trash about to be cleaned out of the basement of a Finnish-American social club to which he belonged. It once had boasted a marching band and this was one of the instruments the club had purchased. I could have it real cheap, he promised. He didn't know what sort of tuba it was, but we established that it was not a sousaphone but some kind of honest-to-God tuba. He would get it for me over the next weekend. On Monday morning I checked with him; he reported the junkman had already been there—the tuba was gone.

I began to despair of ever finding my tuba. I had long since given up the dealers, and all other leads seemed worthless. Then a business associate who had bought a number of instruments for his sons, including a tuba, told me to call a certain musical-instrument store and ask for the owner, Max. He told me Max knew everything about the music business, and I soon came to believe it. The impression of him that I got over the phone was of a little, balding, middle-aged man, in a dingy second-floor showroom, surrounded by large glass cases full of instruments. This would be a fascinating place to people such as me; full of musical bric-a-brac. Max was very pleasant and sympathetic—but he had no used tubas and hadn't had any for a long time. He just laughed when I suggested he put my name on his waiting list for a used tuba.

"Tubas are too big and too expensive. People don't bring them in to sell. They just keep them around the house forever. The only way to find a used tuba," he told me, "is to call the families of deceased tuba players, and see if they will sell the old man's horn."

For a second or two this seemed like very sound advice, but then I realized I had no source whatsoever of names of deceased tuba players. I broached this problem to Max. "Oh, just a moment," he replied. "Let me look in my card file."

He came up with the names of two musicians, both of whom had shuffled off their mortal, and metal, coils within the past year, and both decidedly of Italian extraction if their names meant anything. Apparently the Italians have a great and sincere appreciation of the grandeur of the tuba, an emotion I share wholeheartedly with them. According to Max, one man had owned a Conn; the other had owned a King and something else, possibly another Conn. (The outrageous pun King-Conn went through my mind repeatedly at this time.)

Despite my great desire for a tuba, it took several weeks to screw up enough courage to call these bereaved families. As Max had pointed out to me, the old man's tuba has great sentimental value to his family. It is tangible evidence of a hard-working man; the thing that put the kids through school. My only hope was that one of the families would either want the money or need the space. (I have since found that trying to find storage space for a tuba is about like trying to berth the *Queen Elizabeth* in the Gowanus Canal.)

To my relief, I could not find the name of the first man in the phone book—his family had apparently moved away. I was to be spared the ordeal of that call. Max, however, was acquainted with Alphonso, the son of the second man, and had given me his phone number. I put off calling him as long as possible, then finally gave him a ring one Sunday morning when my wife was taking the kids to Sunday school. It was somehow better to do this without an audience. Al, the owner of his father's two tubas, was not at home. When I explained that I was interested in buying a tuba, his wife asked me to call back in half an hour. She seemed strangely eager for me to do so. A good sign? I called again and got Al.

"I have some string basses I'd like to sell," he told me. "And I have two tubas but they're not for sale. Would you like to come over and see them?"

That was my cue. We made a date for two thirty that afternoon. I assured my family I was only going to "look." I can't remember eating Sunday dinner. About two, I went out the front door, to "look" at tubas—with a blank check in my pocket.

One was a bell-forward King, partially silver-plated. It was long and thin, and its general configuration made me immediately apathetic. The other was an old, short, fat, brass, upright, American-style, B-flat tuba. It was mottled with green corrosion and a white residue of polish that had been applied to it in some earlier era. It had been made by the Grand Rapids Band Instrument Company, in God-only-knows what year. It looked lovely. Could I persuade Al to sell it to me, or did he really mean they weren't for sale?

I explained to Al that I had two places to play such a horn; the concert band and the Dixieland band. He began trying to convince me that the old brass upright was really the proper horn for what I had in mind. Since he was going into the hospital the following day for a two-week stay, I gave him a deposit and took the horn home with me. We had not agreed on the final price. I was to show the horn to a music teacher I know for his opinion of its worth, and I was also to check with Max, to insure that Al was getting a fair deal. I was to call Al again after he came out of the hospital.

I remember driving home with extreme caution lest a bump in the road damage the prize in the back of the car. No one saw me drive in the driveway, park in the carport, remove the tuba from the back seat, and carry it quietly into the house. The tuba was in a dark-green corduroy bag which covered it completely but had no handle; it was necessary to clutch it with both arms. In its bag, carried in this manner, it resembled nothing so much as a body about to be thrown into a lake. I headed for the bedroom, which for some reason seemed the proper place to take it. In the narrow hall, just outside the bedroom door, the first member of my family spotted me, and the others came running. The tuba was disrobed then and there. It was tooted, first by me and then by each member of my family. Eventually we moved into the living room where there was more light and more space. My wife produced a can of silver polish and a no-longer-used diaper, and we alternately played it and polished it for the rest of the afternoon.

The rest is anticlimax. During the next two weeks of unrelieved suspense I checked with my music-teacher friend who approved the price I had offered Al and suggested some slight repair work on the horn; I wondered if Al and I could agree on a price; I checked with Max, who found the figure fair to both parties. And all the time I worried that Al might not sell, after all. My wife announced that she approved the purchase and that *she* would learn to play it. She has since bought some brass polish and done a good job of cleaning it. She has, however, made no progress at all toward learning to play it. We have had to move half my clothes into her closet in order to make a place for it in my closet.

Al stayed in the hospital for two days longer than he predicted and then, the price agreed upon and paid, the tuba was finally mine.

I soon made triumphal entries at rehearsals of both bands.

At the end of my conversation with Max, I tried my best to thank him profusely for the lead. "Think nothing of it," he said. "Drop in sometime and buy a bottle of valve oil."

Then I said something which apparently hadn't occurred to him: "Max, you'd better put my name in your card file, so if anything happens to me, you'll know where to send the next fellow who comes along looking for a used tuba." Max laughed, but I'm sure my name is in his file. After all, the only way to find a used tuba is to call the families of deceased tuba players and see if they will sell the old man's horn.

James J. Faran, Jr., an electronics engineer, lives in Massachusetts with his wife, four children, and a Great Pyrenees dog named Max, who is about the same size as his B-flat tuba.

A Seizure of Limericks

By CONRAD AIKEN

The limerick's, admitted, a verse form;
A terse form, a curse form, a hearse form;
    As pale and as frail
    As the shell of a snail,
It's a whale of a tail in perverse form.

Said Isolde to Tristan: How curious!
King Mark is becoming quite furious.
    Since we got off that boat
    It's been *all "Liebestod"*!
Is it *possible* Wagner is spurious?

Said a Point being approached by a Locus:
I regard this as sheer hocus-pocus.
    What good will it do me
    If it never gets to me?
Will someone *please* tell it to *focus*?

I don't give a hoot, said a particle,
If I can't have the definite article.
    If *cogito sum*
    Pronounces my doom,
Then down with all systems Descartes-ical!

Said a lovely Greek muse known as Clytie
I look very nice in my nighty,
    But beyond all compare,
    I look better when bare,
And when I am bare I am bitey.

Farewell to the old days of Genesis.
We do all these things now by synthesis.
    And who would not rather
    Have a test tube for father
Than a *homo in loco parenthesis*?

Lithpt a thad little man from Duluth
I've got a thore tooth and itth loothe.
    What I needth a Martini
    With O, jutht a teeny,
Or even not any, vermouth.

A lovely young lass in Sesuit
Was in love with a lad from Cotuit.
    Said the preacher from Wareham
    Who proceeded to pair 'em
"Sesuit-Cotuit go to it!"

The Limerick, to put it mildly, is an art form of no great repute. The vast majority of limericks are not intended—even assuming that they are fit—to be printed. They are remembered, and passed on by memory from one *aficionado* to the next, to enliven a dull occasion (or ruin a good one by stopping all other forms of conversation) and eventually to form a part of the folk memory of the race. Periodically attempts are made to collect and (*sub rosa*) publish the unpublishable limericks, ranging in time from *Cythera's Hymnal* of 1870 to the awesomely scholarly and complete *The Limerick: 1,700 Examples, with Notes, Variants, and Index*, brought out by Gershon Legman in 1953. Now and then a poet of stature essays the limerick, seeking to do the impossible and make something more of the printable examples than the master, Edward Lear, could make of them. One such daring renovator is Conrad Aiken, eminent winner of many poetry prizes (see "The Literary Prize Game," HORIZON, July, 1963), who has delivered himself of the limericks on these pages—in an unusual circumstance. They were, he writes, "the immediate result of a coronary which I suffered last February in Savannah. For some inexplicable reason I at once had a seizure of limericks, beginning the day after the attack, and at the rate, for a while, of two or three a day—my wife took them down. It was, I suppose the psychologists would say, the attempt of the unconscious to keep me amused, and it worked very well."

All's quiet along the Potomac.
The Skybolt's asleep with the Bomarc.
    The Kennedy sings
    To the last of the kings
And the diplomat fills his *estomac.*

A delectable gal from Augusta
Vowed that nobody ever had bussed her.
    But an expert from France
    Took a bilingual chance
And the mixture of tongues quite nonplused her.

Nan, Saw, and Paw, of Setucket,
Between them had only one bucket.
    Nan took it and ran
    And the trouble began:
Sawtucket, Pawtucket, Nantucket.

Great archers, and hitters of bull's-eyes!
You wingers of wren's eyes and gull's eyes,
    Ulysses and Tell,
    And Achilles as well!
Where stalk you now baring your skull's eyes?

There was once a wicked young minister
Whose conduct was, shall we say, sinister.
    By methods nightmarish
    He seduced his whole parish,
Except for one squamous old spinister.

I'm a most highly literate cat.
I've had my Litt. D., and all that.
    When in New York, my dear,
    And I read "Litter here,"
Why, I litter at once, and then scat!

There was an old party named Cassidy
Who was famed far and wide for mendacity.
    When asked did he lie,
    He replied: To reply
Would be to impugn his veracity.

Said a curve: I'm becoming hysterical.
It is hell to be merely numerical.
    I bend and I bend,
    But where will I end
In a world that is hopelessly spherical?

Until now man has been up against Nature; from now on he will be up against his own nature. Let us pass over the backward countries where man is still engaged in his agelong struggle against poverty. It is a hard fight, but one for which man is well equipped. How else would a poor animal, almost toothless and clawless, have risen to the status of civilized industrial man in something like one third of the world, if not because of his indomitable fighting spirit? Let us look instead to the far more puzzling and even distressing problems which arise in the advanced countries, where the struggle is won, or almost won.

The victory over poverty is so recent that far too little thought has been given to it. Most people will indignantly deny that the battle is as good as over. The newspapers are full of industrial disputes; the labor unions claim their share, and usually more than their share, of the annual increase of productivity, which is now at the rate of 2–7 per cent in the industrial countries. They try to represent the present state as unbearable hardship, even if it is twice as good as it was twenty-five years ago. These disputes, unless they lead to disastrous strikes, are of course powerful tools of material progress. The pressure of the wage

DRAWINGS BY DAVID LEVINE

The Perils of Leisure

By DENNIS GABOR

earners was, and often still is, necessary to overcome inertia in applying new methods of production. In this day-to-day turmoil people seldom become aware that the battle is now being fought on a different level. One can object that great poverty still exists, even in the United States. But as J. K. Galbraith has shown in his book *The Affluent Society*, this poverty is *pathological*; it is of the same nature as the 3–5 per cent illiteracy which still exists in Britain after nearly a hundred years of compulsory education.

Yet we cannot afford to allow the potentially almost unlimited productivity of modern technology to give an unprepared hu-

manity more leisure than it knows how to use. Moses showed the Promised Land to his people, but then he led them around for forty years in the wilderness, until a new generation had grown up, worthy of it. Forty years appears as a not unreasonable estimate for educating a new generation, which can live in leisure, but we must find a better equivalent of the "wilderness." We have only to look around us to see that it has been found, by the instinctive wisdom of the social body. To put it crudely, it is *unnecessary work* and *waste*. It is not a new invention. General Cavaignac practiced it in 1848. When after the Paris revolution

Once the many toiled in order to serve the few; but soon, when productivity triumphs and automation does away at last with drudgery, work will be the privilege of a tiny minority. Can we adapt to the terrors of such a world?

there was dangerous unrest and unemployment among the workmen, he had ditches dug by one gang and had them filled up by another gang. The invention is not new, but it has been greatly improved. In one of its modern forms it is known as Parkinson's Law: the proliferation of bureaucracy, where anybody at a desk can always give work to somebody at another desk, whether the exchange of paper is productive or not. Compulsory work is on the way out, but *compulsive work* will have to stay with us until a new generation grows up, for whom there will be no sharp limit between work and play.

Modern production has fantastically exceeded the bare necessities. In the eighteenth century some 85 per cent of the population had to grow food, and spun and wove their coarse clothing in the winter. Today in the United States 8.7 per cent of the population produce so much food that millions are on a slimming diet and food sufficient for millions goes daily down the drain; much is exported to needy countries, yet a considerable part of the harvest has to be stored every year to protect the farmers from ruin. Thus the modern industrial state must encourage waste to keep people working. But why must they keep working? Partly

"Man . . . must be adapted to leisure, and his work must become occupational therapy. It must . . . give him the feeling that he is useful and even creative."

because the economic system is traditionally biased so as to pay more for a greater effort rather than for an increased output. But ultimately because, as C. E. M. Joad said, "work is the only occupation yet invented which mankind has been able to endure in any but the smallest possible doses."

This ultimate psychological reason is still mostly below the level of consciousness. From the beginning of industrial civilization very few people have liked work. They work to live; living for work has become conscious only in a small intellectual and administrative elite. To quote Joad again: "If the businessman plays golf, it is, as he will tell you, to keep himself fit for business; if he takes a holiday, he is submitting to boredom for the same reason." The rest would vote for a perpetual holiday—because they have never tried it. Unaware of the fact that work, though far from an enjoyable habit, has become a compulsive habit with them, they would protest their innocence of having helped to create a system which can run only by keeping a maelstrom of paper and goods milling around and down into a gigantic drain.

The rationalizing of clerical work, which is just starting, on

top of the improvement of production methods, which has been going on for a long time and is still accelerating, is bound to produce unemployment in the short run—and *social uselessness* of a large fraction of humanity in the long run. Unemployment may be a matter for social administration; one can always create artificial employment by methods such as those of General Cavaignac or by the more refined methods described by Parkinson. But administrative measures, however refined, will not change the fact that people artificially employed are socially useless; this can be altered only by changing the most fundamental conventions of our civilization.

An industrial civilization has no economic use whatever for people in the lowest ten percentiles, with an IQ below 80, who not so long ago would have been fit to earn their keep as lamplighters, navvies (laborers), swineherds, etc. Lamps are lit automatically, a bulldozer replaces a hundred navvies, and pigs are kept in pens. As Norbert Wiener is wont to say, there is really no place in modern industry for anybody below an IQ of about 110, just as there is no place in a modern army for people below NCO intelligence, that is to say, below the top quarter of the population. Taken as a whole, an industrial civilization still has some use for the 55 per cent of the population between an IQ of 80 and 110, as laborers, low-grade clerks, milkmen, and postmen. These positions appear secure against automation.

There is at present no difficulty in finding jobs for the upper quarter of the population, and there is intense competition for the top 5 per cent, those above an IQ of 126.5. They are badly needed as administrators, lawyers, physicians, engineers, and scientists. All industrial countries are crying out for more and more of these.

To sum up the situation, until quite recently the majority of people had to work to support a leisured minority. For the first time in history we are now faced with the possibility of a world in which only a minority need work, to keep the great majority in idle luxury. Soon the minority which has to work for the rest may be so small that it could be recruited entirely from the gifted part of the population. The rest will be socially useless by the standards of our present-day civilization, founded on what William James called the "Gospel of Work."

One way out of course would be to arrest technological development, or even to retreat a few steps, without going the whole way of Erewhon, in Samuel Butler's utopian novel of that name, and destroying all machines. It is part of the solution in Huxley's *Brave New World*, in which one third of the population is kept on the land—and the production methods are arrested at the stage where they provide seven and a half hours daily work for everybody—while they are made to believe that the methods used are the most progressive possible. The work is so graded that all the various levels of intelligence—which have become separate breeds: Alphas, Betas, Gammas, Deltas, and Epsilons (semi-morons)—are usefully occupied in "congenial" jobs.

Huxley's brilliant satire would not have created such violent revulsion in almost all intellectuals, including Huxley himself, and killed all utopias for thirty years, if it had not contained an element of inescapable truth. This is that we cannot let technology run away with us if we are to survive. We cannot let labor-saving and thought-saving devices proliferate to the point where the large majority of mankind can be kept in nervous equilibrium only by conditioning and by lies.

Man must be brought into equilibrium with his new environment. He must be adapted to leisure, and his work must become *occupational therapy*. It must not only entertain him (this is relatively easy) but keep him mentally alert and give him the feeling that he is useful and even creative. We shall never reach this goal merely by improving push-button machinery.

In such a world, if we can ever achieve it, there will be no need to lie to people to explain why labor-saving devices are not used to reduce their work from, say, six hours to four—or to two, or to nothing. They can take it in the same spirit as they now take the advice of the doctor who tells them they must take more exercise than suits their natural laziness. Better still, they may take it in a sporting spirit. Once the limits between work and play are not as sharply defined as they are now, a certain conservatism in work will become as natural as it is in sport. The high jumper or the sprinter is not supposed to use jet propulsion—and he does not ask for it.

If we want to achieve such a world, we shall need much intelligence and even more charity. The leading minority must forget that the majority are "objectively" useless because they can be replaced by machines. They must find their reward in the happiness of the common man, in a paternal feeling which must never show itself in paternalism. As Huxley said, "Happiness is a hard master—particularly other people's happiness."

I feel that most thinking people will share my horror at the idea of a vastly overpopulated world living on fish rations, in huge tenements, so crowded that they cannot all take their exercise at the same time. I do not expect that everybody will be with me if I declare my preference for a world population of one billion, living on steak and pheasant (or their vegetarian equivalents), rather than for one of 30 or 100 billion, feeding on soya beans and Chlorella, under a strict discipline which reduces personal freedom to a crippled minimum.

I will also state that I wish for a future world in which people will sing and laugh spontaneously when they go to work, and when they return from work. A world in which there is much happiness for the common man, and much creative struggle for the uncommon man.

*F*or the common man, as I want to define him, life is a cycle. It starts with the discovery of the world around the child in which everything is new, it then goes on to the great discoveries of sex and love, and culminates in the young family. It contains the smaller cycles of work, rest, and recreation, of modest wishes and their fulfillment. It can be a happy life to the end if there is not much physical suffering, and if the old man or woman has learned to love the new generation more than himself.

Far be it from me to believe that people need nothing more than material comfort, but I must begin with the problem of pro-

duction. Forty years ago Bertrand and Dora Russell estimated that if all waste and extravagances were cut out, an average of four hours' work per day would be sufficient to produce the goods which at that time were considered necessary for a "good life." This estimate still stands as a reasonable one, though the technological progress in the meantime would now allow us to include in the "good life" many things that were considered luxuries forty years ago. On the other hand we have not got a single step nearer to cutting out waste. The average hours in industry have dropped in the advanced countries from something like sixty hours per week to about forty, and real income has at least doubled; but the waste in armaments, unnecessary transport, obsolescent goods, and Parkinsonian office work has increased all the time.

Even if one disregards the revolutionary changes which may come about by cutting out waste, one is driven to the conclusion that the material paradise of the common man cannot be far away. It is true that in 1962 the New York electricians obtained an official twenty-five-hour week. This, however, means a minimum of thirty hours' actual work, the extra five to be paid at overtime rates. There is every indication that on the way from a forty-hour week to a *real* thirty-hour week there will be a formidable hurdle to take—psychological rather than economic.

By 1976 the gross national product in the U.S.A. can be expected to rise, according to Morris Ernst and other forecasters, to 800 billion dollars, and the population to 190 million. Personal consumption may reach 500 billion dollars, amounting to more than 10,000 dollars per family, about three times more than in 1929 at the height of the first great American boom. Lest it might be objected that this will be consumed "by the rich," it appears likely that by 1976 the "workers," even in the narrowest sense of the term, may receive perhaps 80 per cent of the national income, especially if one considers that workers are also stockholders and receivers of interest on their savings.

How does the worker in the United States spend his money? Most of it of course goes into food, clothing, housing—primary necessities, though satisfied far above the traditional level—and into new "necessities" such as automobiles; but some 11 per cent goes into recreation. Not surprisingly, a huge industry has grown up in the U.S. to cater to the leisure of the common man. According to Ernst, 3.5 billion dollars were spent on "do-it-yourself" tools and materials in 1953, of which not less than 150 million were spent on power tools. Many Americans have a real little factory in their homes, and play at work after "working hours." A billion and a quarter per year now goes into photography. Billions are spent on pleasure boats, of which there are already seven and a quarter million, used by 40 million people. At least 3 billion dollars are spent on foreign travel, and a fourth as much on pets. Passive entertainment takes a comparable sum: 1.8 billion on theatres and movies, almost three times as much on television and radio. The sale of phonograph records has shot up to half a billion, a quarter of which is for classical music. With this we have reached the fringe of what is traditionally called "culture."

What of ambition? At its most absurd one may read the lower

class of American science fiction of the "space opera" type, in which high-energy individuals fight it out with one another as the heads of "interplanetary trusts." But as John Maynard Keynes foresaw thirty years ago, the "economic game" is now losing its attraction. Nowadays, university-educated young Britishers seldom want to get rich—only comfortably well off—and even in the United States the millionaire is no longer the hero he used to be. It becomes increasingly easy to make a living, more difficult to make a fortune, and the young people seem to adapt themselves to this situation, though with a visible loss of zest. This process will go on, but it must not be allowed to lead to complete apathy. Mankind will need a moral equivalent of the economic game, as it now needs—again in William James's phrase—a "moral equivalent of war."

*S*ooner or later we must ask whether the common man can be happy in a world in which his security is assured, and in which his time is spent between mild work, designed at least as much as occupational therapy as for the production of goods, and healthy recreation. Few people would have doubted this fifty years ago, an affirmative answer would still be considered self-evident in Russia or in China, but grave doubts have arisen in the advanced Western countries. Thirty years ago George Orwell declared his love for the proletariat, and delighted in the picture of the proletarian family with "father sitting in his shirt sleeves at the fire, reading the newspaper." Would he have liked the picture of father with his eyes glued to the television screen, with a small car in his garage? I doubt it.

There are today five million compulsive alcoholics in the United States, a ratio equalled only by Sweden. The rate is highest in the West, which by climate and wealth is the nearest thing to an industrial paradise. In lovely San Francisco one adult male in ten is an alcoholic. In criminality the U.S. has the highest rate of all countries. In Britain between 1939 and 1961 crimes of violence by the 14–21 age group have increased about fifteenfold. This, writes Anthony Crosland, "came as a particularly poignant shock to liberals who had traditionally equated crime with poverty and bad housing: the new violence, on the contrary, seemed actually a product of prosperity."

The more permissive the society, the less permissive must be the education which makes the individual fit to live in it. If the adult is not to abuse his freedom, self-discipline must be impressed into the moldable character of the child or adolescent. Some of the more successful of the old privileged classes had an inkling of this: witness the harshness of the old English public schools or the spartan upbringing of the samurai. Those who lacked this instinct, like the French nobles of the *ancien régime*, perished by violence—if they had not died first from boredom.

In the first years of childhood probably not much harshness will be needed to educate citizens for the Age of Leisure. But there can be little doubt that hardship will be a necessary component in the education of the adolescent. William James expressed this clearly in 1910, in his famous address with "The Moral Equivalent of War" as its subject:

If now—and this is my idea—there were, instead of military conscription a conscription of the whole youthful population to form for a certain number of years a part of the army enlisted against *Nature*, the injustice would tend to be evened out, and numerous other goods to the Commonwealth would follow. . . . To coal and iron mines, to freight trains, to fishing fleets in December, to dishwashing, clothes-washing and window washing, to road-building and tunnel-making, to foundries and stoke holes and to the frames of skyscrapers, would our gilded youths be drafted off, according to their choice, to get the childishness knocked out of them and to come back into society with healthier sympathies and soberer ideas.

For a long time to come it will be possible to make the Peace Corps useful in the old sense, by sending young men to underdeveloped countries, but later on it will become a pure Hardship Course, with ample social justification without being productive in goods. H. G. Wells made such a course a part of the education of the guardians in his *Modern Utopia*, the "samurai," but it will be equally indispensable for the common man of the future. H. G. Wells's worthiest present-day successor, the Russian paleontologist I. Yefremov, the most distinguished of Soviet science-fiction writers, calls the hardship course "herculean tasks." Every young man and woman in his utopian world must perform feats on a truly heroic scale, such as "building a water supply for a North Tibetan mine, replant an Araucaria forest on the Nehebt plateau in South America, and exterminate the sharks which have again made their appearance at the coast of Australia." (As these are the labors which *one* of his heroes had to do when he was a young man, one wonders what is left for the others?) It is not surprising though that a present-day Russian, however superior to his contemporaries in courage or imagination, could not break himself of the Gospel of Work, and that he lets his youths fight on the limited front against Nature, like William James. The time is still far off when the Gospel of Work can be debunked in Russia.

In the past the common man has found his greatest joy and fulfillment in the family. I will take it for granted that for a very long time to come the family will remain the basic unit of society. So many things must change in the future that men and women will hang on to the familiar institution of monogamous marriage, as well as to the institutionalized religions. The large family is now threatened; nay, it has become impossible by the progress of medical science, which does not allow more than 2.15 babies per family in a stationary population. Add to this the fact that the average length of life has now increased to 70.2 years, and may well increase further when greater scientific effort is concentrated on senescence. As the age at marriage and at the birth of the children is decreasing in the industrially advanced countries, the time is coming when rearing a family will occupy less than one half of the parents' adult life. I can see a way of reconciling these hard facts with the natural wish of people to be surrounded by children, but it is a hard way.

The small suburban house, the emblem of our civilization, is like a bird's nest; it is meant to rear the offspring, not to hold the generations together. When the children have gone out into the world, the parents are left alone. A *real* family house was once the finest reward of success; it gave the parents a sort of immortality to live with their children and grandchildren. The family and the family house had their finest development in China, as one can read in that bewitching book, *The House of Exile*, by Nora Waln. This is now destroyed—in China deliberately, because the all-powerful state could not tolerate strong family loyalties. In the Western world it was destroyed not deliberately, but partly because of the greater mobility of population required by industrial life and partly by that spirit of independence which makes young people intolerant of parents and absolutely intolerant of in-laws.

Far too few people seem to have realized how great an old-world value we have thrown away by making a bird's nest of the family house, and these few are mostly reactionaries. I want to ask: Is there really no possibility of bringing back the permanent, multigeneration family and its material union, the large family house? I know the psychological obstacles appear prohibitive; in the present climate of opinion in the English-speaking countries two women, especially two in-laws, can hardly live together under one roof. But climates of opinion can be changed, and the gain would be enormous not only for the happiness of the older people but also for our culture. The modern suburb is certainly better than workers' slums, but a population housed in the modern version of stately homes, in large country houses with ample grounds, is something to fire the imagination.

Travel, hobbies, passive enjoyment of the arts, may be feeble substitutes to lonely, elderly people for the feeling of immortality which the family can give, but a steady intellectual and spiritual growth in the age of postmaturity can be more than a compensation for lost youth. Unfortunately, it is given to few people, of whom Goethe was the supreme example. Can it be within the reach of the common man of the future? Until there is a revolutionary development in the technique of education, only a fraction of the population—let us say 10 per cent—can participate intellectually in our civilization, instead of just *living* in it, as strangers. It is probably this fraction, and not many more, who are able to understand modern science. One can add to them a probably larger fraction of those who cannot understand science but who derive an intense enjoyment from art, practiced or passively enjoyed. These groups, probably not more than a quarter of our population, are those for whom the way to continued intellectual development in their age of postmaturity may be open.

My idea of the amateur scientist is that he shall be a *knower*, not a *doer*. This type has become very rare in our research-minded world. Not so very long ago meetings of the British Association for the Advancement of Science used to be visited by lawyers, clergymen, and country gentlemen who liked to be up-to-date, but their number is dropping from year to year. Of course, nowadays it is much more difficult for the laymen to get up to date—but all the better for those who have the true spirit of curiosity. The years which may be needed to master relativity, quantum mechanics, astrophysics, protein chemistry, genetics,

will make it a worthwhile achievement. Why should an amateur scientist not be sixty or seventy before he acquires a thorough and universal understanding of science, and then feel as happy as the Chinese scholar did when he could pass his Mandarin examination at seventy-five?

"Take three hundred men out of history and we should still be living in the Stone Age." One might object to this dictum of Sir Arthur Keith that it is not proven that if the three hundred great innovators had not lived there would not have been others to take their places a little later. But make it ten thousand or even a hundred thousand instead of three hundred; it still remains true that without an exceedingly small minority of uncommon men the vast mass of humanity would have remained inert. Today one can say though, with equal truth, "Add half a dozen uncommon men of the type and power of a Napoleon or a Hitler to the history of the next century, and the chances are that we shall once more be living in the Stone Age."

At the present juncture of history we can no longer afford to have uncommon men with demoniac power and with the morals of adolescent gangsters. In the past such men were often pow-

"Why should an amateur scientist not be sixty or seventy before he acquires a thorough and universal understanding of science?"

erful ferments of history; in the long run the good they left behind sometimes outweighed the bad. At the present time the evil they could do would be so overwhelming that it is a very academic question whether historians of the future (if there are any historians left) will give them a few good marks. "Whoever wishes to rule over slaves is himself a runaway slave," wrote Walther Rathenau, an early martyr of Nazism. It may not be true that all men are born free, but they can certainly be educated to be free. A few generations away from slavery tyrannical power becomes unbearable not only to the ruled, it also becomes unattractive to those who in more primitive civilizations would have become power addicts. This is not starry-eyed optimism; anybody can observe that in the old, stable democracies the tyrannical ruler has become a thing of the past, and also the tyrannical husband or father. But in the greater part of the world people are not more than one generation away from slavery, and for at least another generation we shall be in a danger zone.

Escape from this danger zone means that history as we know it will come to an end; history in terms of wars and conquests. It means also the coming of the world of "*post-historic man*"; of the common man living for his own happiness, not for the glorification of his rulers, and of the uncommon man who finds his fulfillment in enriching the life of the common man. Let us not conceal from ourselves the strongly ambivalent reaction which this provokes in us. We have all been brought up on history; as children we have all identified ourselves with one or the other of the national heroes. There is a little answering echo in most of us to the words of that Fascist professor who said: "We do not want a cause to live for, we want a cause to die for!" (I wish I knew whether he died with Mussolini?) It is easy to smile at the Fascist professor; it is easy to say that we have learned history the wrong way, and that we ought to have been taught enthusiasm for the (unknown) inventor of the iron plow rather than for the Black Prince. It will take more than just rational, humanistic education to overcome the irrational longing for archaic adventure.

In our Western society this is instinctively understood and dealt with, not unsuccessfully, in an empirical way. Catharsis has become big business. The cinema industry treats us periodically

"Mozartian man . . . the creator whose art does not live on conflict, who creates for joy, out of joy."

to more and more splendid and gory reconstructions of the horrors of past wars and of the horrors of Calvary. In peaceful Britain there are more than a hundred murders per year, but at least fifteen hundred are committed in the crime thrillers. Nobody can say exactly how successful these channels are for the vicarious satisfaction of aggressive instincts. There are those who blame violence in motion pictures and in television for the alarming rise in juvenile delinquency, but nobody has been able to prove that it is mainly the movie, television, and thriller addicts who become criminals. I am rather inclined to agree with Bertrand Russell that "the man who kills his wife with every circumstance of cruelty is a public benefactor by vicariously relieving thousands of their aggressive instincts." This is probably true for the antisocial instincts which break out in individual crime, but I believe it to be untrue of the glorification of war and of nationalistic instincts which break out in collective crime. The instinct which seeks an outlet in a "just war" is just as archaic and out-of-place as the adrenal mechanism of the body which makes the muscles supple during an examination in mathematics.

If we are to indoctrinate people with the belief that history must come to an end, then we shall need something better than the cathartic industry, or the "violent passion surrogate" of the Huxley of 1931, or the mountaineering and tree-chopping of the Huxley who published *Island*, a revision of *Brave New World*, in 1962. This is one of the great tasks for the uncommon man of the future. It is not simply the problem of making man a more perfectly social animal. The man who wants to sacrifice his life for his nation is highly social, but we shall have no use for him. The loyalty of post-historic man must be for his family—and for the whole of humanity, with nothing between these two extremes but harmless voluntary affiliations, professional groups, brotherhoods, at most political parties.

*S*cience will provide congenial work for uncommon men and women as far as thought can reach. Science itself is based on the unprovable belief that there is order at the basis of natural phenomena, which can be adequately represented by logic. This implies that by digging down into the foundations we shall in the end discover a *finite* set of regular relations, and that the quest for fundamentals must have an end. I repeat that this is unprovable—what is more, it will not be possible to prove that the set of laws of nature is complete even when no phenomena can be reproduced which cannot be accounted for by them, because unknown laws can still be hidden in unique, irreproducible phenomena. But whether the quest for fundamentals is finite or endless, there is no limit in the development of science toward complexity—other than the interest of men in it.

The logical structure of chemistry was essentially laid down by atomism at the beginning of the nineteenth century. The theoretical foundations were later enriched by thermodynamics and quantum theory, but the main development was toward complexity, in a way which would not have surprised its great founders. This development has now reached the stage of "molecular biology," the chemistry of the most complex substances of the living organisms: the proteins and the nucleic acids. For this reason, chemistry has never lacked enthusiastic workers; one can even say that molecular biology is now at the very focus of scientific interest. In the past ten years physics had to yield first place to it. This was expected by many people in the twenties, but then high-energy physics produced one miracle after the other. The atomic nucleus disintegrated into unexpected fragments, yielding some thirty new elementary particles and large fission products, and particles of antimatter popped out of the vacuum. It is likely now that, after some twenty-five years of exciting novelties, high-energy physics will give the theoreticians time to catch up, and the physical-biological sciences will hold the center of the stage for a long time, perhaps to the end of the scientific interests of *Homo sapiens*.

I cannot see men ever losing interest in science as long as they have logical thinking faculties which want to be exercised. It is another question how long science will attract the best talents who in other epochs would probably have become artists, and in the Renaissance both artists and scientists, like Leonardo and

Wren. It has often been predicted that at some time religion, metaphysics, and mysticism may seduce the best intellects. This has indeed happened fairly often in the case of individual scientists, but is has never yet happened to a whole civilization.

Science may be endless, or at any rate its end is nowhere in view, but what about art? How will the arts flourish in a peaceful world without conflict?

This is a grave question indeed. It cannot be denied that the verbal arts, the drama, the novel, and a great part of poetry have always fed on conflict, and that they have reached their greatest heights when the conflict was unresolvable except by a tragic end. Aldous Huxley in his *Island* has given a rational ending to *Oedipus Rex*, but it reads like a parody. How could a Shakespeare or a Tolstoy display his supreme talents in a world in which there is no injustice? Even a humorist would find himself badly hampered in a world in which nothing is out of place—except perhaps banana skins.

This dilemma is keenly felt in our times; it is probably the strongest reason for the hostility of many artists to the future. There is no solution to it; if we abolish injustice we must abolish with it the great art which is based on injustice, on blood and violent death, that "masculine" type of art whose greatest representative in our time was Ernest Hemingway. We shall be able to retain the feminine type, the sensuous and sensitive writers, whether male or female. And one great conflict will always remain with us: the conflict between man's nature and civilization. This need not remain always a malaise expressed with self-pitying neurotic moanings, a la Strindberg; the great artists of the future may be able to sublimate it, and invent a new catharsis—which will reconcile man with his fate to be happy! It will be an art of maturity, which will make the art of the Greek tragedians and of Shakespeare appear to be the writings of gifted adolescents. (I do not deny, though, that there are few mature men who do not have a sneaking envy of adolescence.)

Is this all a dream? Will creative lives be possible in such a future? Immanuel Kant wrote that "in an Arcady all talent would be nipped in the bud," and his acid wisdom has found a strong echo for two centuries. Yet Kant had a contemporary who gave the lie to it.

Wolfgang Amadeus Mozart was a creator fit to live in Arcady. He had a short, hard, and tragic life, but his work owes nothing to his sufferings, everything to his innate rich and happy nature. How few of these blessed angels there have been in the history of culture, compared with the great tormented creators like Michelangelo, Beethoven, Dostoevsky, Flaubert! No wonder that modern criticism tries to reject Eduard Mörike's picture of Mozart as a happy child-genius. I prefer to disbelieve those who want to make a neurotic of him (who has ever reacted with less of a trauma to a physical kick in the seat of his pants?), and I believe that he would have reached just as great heights without a pedantic, exacting father, without the humiliations of the unspeakable archbishop, and without the almost constant worry of debts.

I prefer to believe that Mozart was a forerunner of Mozartian Man, of the creator whose art does not live on conflict, who creates for joy, out of joy. It is hard to imagine a Mozart born and bred among our "dark satanic mills," and what is worse, in a society devoted to the Gospel of Work. When the simple man and woman will often feel that "the heart jumps in your bosom with joy"—*"nel seno vi bulica il core,"* as Zerlina sings in *Don Giovanni*—in that world Mozarts may be born again.

But beyond this? Let me quote what Bertrand Russell had to say in one of those rare moments when the great skeptic tried to force himself into enthusiasm: "There is no reason why, in the ages to come, the sort of man who is now exceptional should not become usual, and if that were to happen, the exceptional man in that new world would rise as far above Shakespeare as Shakespeare now rises above the common man."

Modern man in the West has been kept going for a long time now by the Gospel of Work and by the Bitch Goddess Success. The Gospel of Work is now enthusiastically adopted by the East, too, though the Bitch Goddess has been decorously draped as Collective Success. No wonder that in such a world the few idlers, the playboys and playgirls of the Riviera and of other golden beaches, behave little better than slaves at the Saturnalia. The good citizen can afford *dolce far niente* only after he retires, and tries to enjoy the world through soured eyes as he goes on a long cruise with his aging wife. Many such citizens wish that they had been allowed to die in harness.

"Education for Leisure" is a modern slogan, with little solid substance behind it for the time being. What else can one expect in the case of a movement which appears to stand in direct opposition to the Gospel of Work? The least controversial aspect of it is the care for the old people, for those who have done their work. It is only a matter of common humanity to offer passive recreation to the old and infirm. There is a snobbish stigma attached to passive enjoyment; it is condemned by the intellectuals when it is "gluing the eyes to the television screen," but one hears no such condemnation of listening to Bach or reading the *Lives* of Plutarch. One is as passive as the other, though admittedly Bach or Plutarch is more likely to lead to active contemplation in minds which are fit for it. But it is too late to encourage contemplation after a life spent in hard work.

Education for leisure must start much earlier, and it would be more properly called education for happiness in a complex civilization. We cannot be satisfied with anything less than a human race with a vitality equal to that of the best-favored of our young people: "Iron-jointed, supple-sinew'd they shall dive and they shall run," and they shall make love equally naturally and instinctively, they shall also make music out of the sheer joy of life; they shall understand man's fate and be proud to be men.

Dennis Gabor, physicist, engineer, and inventor, is Professor of Applied Electron Physics at the Imperial College of Science and Technology in the University of London. This article will form a part of his book, Inventing the Future, *to be published by Alfred A. Knopf, Inc., this coming January.*

OBEYING THE LAW

The most blindingly dull law can create the finest art form. In the eyes of the law, for example, a fire escape may simply be an "egress," but for the Australian photographer John Drake it is a pattern which permits extemporizing, a set of variations on the theme of floor and stair, a source of ever-changing geometric patterns in light and shadow. Mr. Drake started with a fire escape in Hoboken and has since photographed many more in the New York vicinity.

Sub-Article 7. Fire Escapes

(6.7.1). § C26-298.0 **Construction of Fire Escapes.**—When fire escapes are used as a means of egress under the provisions of section C26-276.0, such fire escapes shall be constructed of incombustible materials and shall be of sufficient strength to sustain safely a superimposed load of one hundred pounds per square foot. Fire escapes used as a means of egress shall have balconies at each story. Such balconies shall be at least thirty-six inches wide in the clear and at least fifty-four inches long, and shall be provided with staircases extending to the ground level with a maximum riser of eight inches and a minimum width of treads of eight inches exclusive of nosings. Fire escape staircases shall be at least twenty-two inches in width. If fire escapes are located on a street front of a structure, the superintendent may permit the use of a drop ladder or a counterbalanced stair from the lowest balcony, provided that the height of such balcony above the sidewalk is sixteen feet or less.

(6.7.2). § C26-298.1 **Fire Escapes; Certain Requirements.**—Drop ladders where permitted shall be provided with guides and hooks of a type satisfactory to the department. All fire escapes unless of non-corrodible metal shall be painted and shall be maintained in good condition and free from rust and corrosion. Notice shall be given to the superintendent by the owner prior to the painting of fire escapes whether or not such painting is done to remove a violation.

(6.7.2). § C26-299.0 **Party Wall Balconies.**—Party wall balconies may be used as an auxiliary means of egress on structures erected before January first, nineteen hundred thirty-eight, if the property on both sides of such party and fire wall is under the same ownership and the type of occupancy of both buildings is the same and such balcony is extending to pass a plain glass glazed opening accessible as an emergency exit on either side of such party and fire wall.

(6.7.3). § C26-300.0 **Removal and Obstruction of Party Wall Balconies.**—a. Each of the owners of adjoining structures, commonly served by party wall balconies serving as a required means of egress, shall maintain that portion of each such balcony which is on his property, and each such owner shall maintain egress normally un-obstructed and unimpeded, from each such balcony to and through his structure, except as otherwise provided for in this section.

b. It shall be unlawful for the owner of a structure on which there is a party wall balcony serving as a required means of egress from an adjoining structure, to remove such party wall balcony or any portion thereof or to prevent, eliminate or obstruct egress from such party wall balcony to and through his structure, unless and until such owner has had erected or has obligated himself to erect on the structure deprived of such required means of egress, a legal fire escape or other means of egress approved by the superintendent.

Sub-Article 8. Obstruction of Means of Egress

(6.8). § C26-301.0 **Obstruction of Means of Egress.**—It shall be unlawful to place any obstruction in front of, in or on any required means of egress.

§ C26-301.1 **Obstruction of Certain Means of Egress.**—Fire escapes, exterior stairways, their drop ladders and counterbalanced stairs shall be kept entirely clear of flower boxes, flower pots, chairs, pails and other obstructions. No projecting sign or other projection shall be so placed as to interfere with the free operation or use of any fire-escape drop ladder or any counterbalanced stair, nor shall any projecting sign or other projection be placed within three feet of such drop ladder or counterbalanced stair. No duct shall terminate within ten feet of the course of a fire escape or outside iron stairway.

Sub-Article 9. Special Egress Requirements for Structures of a Public Character

(6.9.1). § C26-302.0 **Provision for Public Safety Under Unusual Conditions Respecting Means of Egress.**—a. Where unusual conditions occur in structures of a public character such as hotels, restaurants, railroad depots, public halls, club houses with more than eight sleeping rooms, churches, ball parks, stadia, opera houses, concert halls, theatres and other similar structures, used or intended to be used for public as-